YESTERDAY
IN
HAWAI'I

A VOYAGE THROUGH TIME

In Hawaiian the plural of lei is nā lei, not the Anglicized leis. Other Hawaiian words that have entered the world vocabulary (hula, aloha, etc.) are italicized.

Published and distributed by

ISLAND HERITAGE™
P U B L I S H I N G

94-411 Kō'aki Street, Honolulu, Hawai'i 96797-2806
Orders: (800) 468-2800 • Information: (808) 564-8800
Fax: (808) 564-8877
islandheritage.com

Soft Cover ISBN: 1-61710-233-4, EAN: 978-1-61710-233-2

Second Edition, Fourth Printing—2016

YESTERDAY IN HAWAI'I

A VOYAGE THROUGH TIME

NEW EDITION

Scott C. S. Stone

ADDITIONAL TEXT BY
Waimea Williams

IMAGE EDITOR
Mazeppa K. Costa

ISLAND HERITAGE™
PUBLISHING

For Simon Cardew,
in memoriam

CONTENTS

INTRODUCTION

The great Polynesian voyages of discovery across the Pacific, beginning with people of the Lapita culture in Southeast Asia some fifteen hundred years before the birth of Christ, and culminating in the discovery of the Hawaiian Islands, were arguably the greatest human dispersal in history. What followed was epic in its own way—Hawai'i came out of a profound isolation to become home for people from all over the world, people who fashioned a society in which all were equal regardless of race. It could not have happened everywhere, and it has hardly happened anywhere.

And Hawai'i, which experienced internecine warfare and political upheavals, did not merely survive but prospered in an aura of equality. The edifice that became a society of equal people was not built in a day, nor was it always easy, but in the end people of goodwill were able to be neighbors and business partners and to court future spouses from a variety of other races.

The influx of foreigners filled the Islands with new and sometimes curious ideas—new music and festivals, foods and customs, and ways of looking at things. New gods came as well, and new commerce—new work to occupy the days. Some uniquely Hawaiian concepts were lost in the rush to progress, but more often there was a kind of Hawaiian patina over the new things, so that Hawaiian concepts and styles did not disappear but were shared among the stream of later immigrants. Hawai'i became a society that celebrated its differences as well as its similarities.

Some years, even some decades, were better than others, but that is the nature of time's passage. Hawai'i has known downtimes of economic woes, often because of influences from beyond the reef. Recessions and labor disputes on the American Mainland have impacted Hawai'i. But there have been great times as well, when people of the Islands knew a lifestyle that others could envy. It is notable that in both good times and bad the people of Hawai'i have maintained an appreciation for their stunning environment, making even the bad times often seem better than conditions and situations in other places.

Hawai'i has developed from a group of chiefdoms into a kingdom, a provisional government, a republic, a territory, and finally a state of the United States. It has known monarchs and pirates, con men and heroes. It is a fragile ecosystem replete with volcanic eruptions, earthquakes, and tsunami, yet somehow it is enduring. Its history is as turbulent as it is colorful. As in any society, however, the ordinary people going about the ordinary business of their lives are what make a community and a history, so it is valuable to look back at the people and their activities to get a sense of time's footfalls. The photographs in this book are snapshots of some of the people and events that help illuminate Hawai'i's yesterdays.

CHAPTER 1

ANCIENT HAWAI'I MEETS THE WESTERN WORLD

At the time when the earth became hot
At the time when the heavens turned about
At the time when the sun was darkened
To cause the moon to shine
The time of the rise of the Pleiades
The slime, this was the source of the earth
The source of the darkness that made darkness
The source of the night that made night
The intense darkness, the deep darkness
Darkness of the sun, darkness of the night
Nothing but night.

–*Kumulipo*, ancient Hawaiian chant on the creation and evolution of life, translated by Martha Beckwith.

The Hawaiians' view of their origins and development is mystical and poetic. It is a view married to a rock-hard pragmatism, for the Polynesians who spread across the Pacific, and in time became Hawaiians, were a practical people, attuned to the earth and the sea. Their story is not one of passive adaptation but one of interaction with new environments and ecosystems. When they sailed from the Marquesas and Tahiti they brought their sustenance—pigs, yams, taro, bananas, breadfruit—sixteen species of crop plants and animals. When they settled in the land they named Hawai'i, they altered the landscape to suit their needs. They used fire to clear fields, diverted streams to make irrigation systems, and built large fishponds.

By the year 1200 the leeward coasts of the main Islands had permanent settlements. By 1400 the leeward areas were being cleared for vast fields of taro and sweet potatoes. It is estimated that by 1600 about 80 percent of all land in Hawai'i below fifteen hundred feet had been altered by human inhabitants.

LEFT: Verdant Hanapēpē Valley on Kaua'i, the first Hawaiian Island to be visited by Cook, 1778, who was first mistaken for the god Lono. However, Westerners brought decades of diseases fatal to Hawaiians. C. Wilkes, 1840.

The Hawaiians were building a civilization, not only by use of the land but also by a steady evolution of language, arts, crafts, and culture. Population swelled to an estimated four hundred thousand as their society grew ever more complex. It was not always a peaceful evolution: as small chiefdoms flourished and the chiefs competed for wider control, the warfare could be merciless.

One important chief brought the strife to an end in 1795 when he completed conquest of all the Islands except Kaua'i, which later came into his kingdom via diplomacy. Kamehameha I was the epitome of what it meant to be a Hawaiian warrior-chief—tough, adaptable, clever, and ruthless. Especially important was his adaptability, for he used Western advisors and guns to complete his conquest.

There is a cogent argument that the Spanish knew Hawai'i, for their ships regularly sailed between Acapulco, Mexico, and the Philippines. Spanish galleons generally sailed north or south of Hawai'i, but a map that a British officer captured from the Spanish in 1742 shows the location of two islands, La Mesa (The Table) and Los Mojas (The Monks), in the latitude and relative longitude where the Hawaiian Islands exist—seemingly irrefutable proof that between the years 1556 and 1778 the Spanish were aware of and perhaps had visited Hawai'i. Furthermore, while the feather capes, headdresses, and weapons of Hawai'i were unknown elsewhere in Polynesia, they bear a striking resemblance to those of Spain. The colors most often used in Hawaiian feather capes were red and gold – Spain's royal colors then and now. Finally, in the 1950s (in the Bishop Museum) a previously unexamined burial casket from old Hawai'i revealed a piece of iron and a piece of cloth believed to be Spanish sailcloth.

In any case, the most historically visible stranger to appear on Hawaiian shores was the renowned explorer Captain James Cook. Born in 1746 of obscure parents in an obscure village in Yorkshire, England, he worked as a farmer and as a clerk in a grocery and a haberdasher's shop, then ran away to sea at eighteen. Strong and intelligent, he worked his way up through the fleet and became perhaps the most famous explorer in the world.

During his third and last voyage, Cook brought his ships into the mid-Pacific. He spotted O'ahu on January 18, 1778, and the next day Kaua'i and Ni'ihau, and he received a friendly reception from the Hawaiians on Kaua'i. He named the isles the Sandwich Islands, after his patron and friend the Earl of Sandwich. Two weeks later he set sail for America, hoping to find the Northwest Passage. When he failed in that endeavor, he sailed the *Resolution* and *Discovery* back to Hawai'i, sighted Maui, and finally anchored in Kealakekua Bay, on the southern shore of the Island of Hawai'i.

Portrait of Captain James Cook, the most highly acclaimed explorer of his time.

The young warrior Kamehameha saw Cook land at Kealakekua, 1779, when the major Islands were controlled by different chiefs. By 1816, when Kamehameha sat for this drawing by Choris, the old warrior was absolute monarch of Hawai'i, Maui, Kaho'olawe, Lāna'i, Moloka'i, O'ahu, and Kaua'i. He had vast lands, absolute authority, and an appreciation of Western guns and ships, and utilized *haole* (foreign, white) counsel.

Queen Ka'ahumanu (1772-1832), the strong-willed, most-favored of Kamehameha's more than 20 wives, became regent at his death, sharing power with Kamehameha II and, later, with Kamehameha III. By motivating Kamehameha II to overturn the *kapu* system, she changed the course of Hawaiian history.

Uniformed in mask-like gourd helmets with foliage and strips of *kapa* (bark cloth), paddlers of a small double-hulled canoe seem to be en route to a ceremonial occasion, accompanied by a *kahuna* (priest) with a carved figure. Engraving after Webber.

Hawaiian figures ranged in size from towering temple images to gods under 12 inches. Made of wood, stone, sea-urchin spine, and net-covered basketry plugged with feathers, their detail elements included pearl shells, human hair, bones, seeds, and dog and shark teeth. Etchings after T. Davies, c. 1800.

"A Man of the Sandwich Islands with His Helmet" (above left) and "A Young Woman of the Sandwich Islands" depict superb feather work worn only by the *ali'i* (nobility) class. Feather helmets, capes, and cloaks were reserved for men; women of rank wore feather *lei* on the head and/or neck. Engravings from Webber, 1779.

At Ahu'ena *heiau*, personal temple of Kamehameha I (Kailua, Hawai'i Island), ritual figures have imposing authority in 1816. Most images and temples came down following abolishment of the *kapu* (prohibition) system just months after Kamehameha's death in 1819. Lithograph after Choris.

"The Death of Captain Cook." Hawaiians had never known Europeans but were aware of iron. They asked for it, accepted gifts of it, and pilfered it. Iron led to the dispute ending in Cook's death, February 14, 1779. His surgeon David Samwell reported that he was "… stabbed in the back of the neck with an iron dagger."

On February 14, 1779, Cook and four marines were killed at Kealakekua in a dispute with Hawaiians over a stolen cutter. It was a terrible tragedy because Cook, more than most early explorers since, liked and respected Hawaiians. He wrote in his journal:

> Few … now lamented our having failed in our endeavor to find a northern passage homeward last summer. To this disappointment we owed our having it in our power to revisit the Sandwich Islands, and to enrich our voyage with a discovery which, though the last, seemed, in every respect, to be the most important that had hitherto been made by Europeans throughout the extent of the Pacific Ocean.

Cook had opened the door, but his death meant that no ships called in Hawai'i for several years, during which time only a handful of Westerners were ashore in the Islands. Marooned British seamen John Young and Isaac Davis became advisors to Kamehameha in the use of Western weapons. Other ships came to deal in sandalwood. The wood was cut in Hawai'i, picked up by Western ships, and transported to Canton, where Chinese craftsmen made marvelous boxes and other artifacts from the fragrant wood. This ushered in the era of the traders, who were entrepreneurs of the most daring kind. Two brothers, Captains Jonathan and Nathan Winship, persuaded Kamehameha to give them a monopoly on sandalwood so he received a quarter of all profits. It was one of the early business arrangements between a leading Hawaiian and men from America, and like some later ones, it did not turn out well for either party. Kamehameha complained that he was being cheated, and the Winship brothers failed to capitalize on the trade.

Four Russian expeditions visited Hawai'i in the early 19th century. Kamehameha and his court received Captain Otto von Kotzebue and officers from the *Rurick*, Kealakekua Bay, November 1816. The Russian government was not interested in establishing colonies in the Islands. Lithograph after Choris.

"*Vue du port hanarourou*," lithograph from Choris, c. 1816. Kamehameha I staunchly upheld Hawai'i's ancient *kapu* system but used the ships and guns of the West. His Honolulu fort at the center here had a coral-stone house, numerous thatch houses, and several of his ships and outrigger canoes.

"A Sandwich Island Officer of the King in Grand Costume" by Arago, August 1819. This proud, ranking chief in exquisite traditional regalia also carries the mark of Western influence. The tattoo on his right arm cites the death of Kamehameha, and his geometric tattoos signify rank and genealogy.

Louis Choris, artist on the *Rurick*, 1816, rendered this "Woman of the Sandwich Islands" with dignity befitting the chiefly rank signified by her *lei hino palaoa* – a neckpiece of braided hair hung with a pendant of carved whale's tooth.

In stark contrast to Choris in the same period, artist Jacques Arago on the *Uranie* illustrated the "Manner of punishing a criminal in the Sandwich Islands," 1819. Sacrificial victims were often selected from *kauwā* (outcast class), whose lives were destined to end as offerings for the gods.

In 1816 the Russian ship *Rurick* visited Hawai'i on a scientific expedition. In Honolulu the artist Choris sketched "*Port d'hanarourou*," an active village still under *kapu* control but adopting Western imports – notably cows and horses.

In 1793 Captain George Vancouver, who had sailed with Cook, brought Hawai'i's first cattle as a present to Kamehameha. As commander of the armed survey ship *Discovery*, Vancouver assumed the role of military advisor to the conquering chief. The captain even arranged a tearful reconciliation between the great warrior and Ka'ahumanu, his willful and favored wife.

HULA, THE DANCE OF LIFE:
BOTH SACRED AND PROFOUND

Hula at the time of early Western contact was a visual rendering and/or enhancement of Hawai'i's oral literature. Without knowledge of Hawai'i's language, poetic conventions, and cultural and religious traditions, it was impossible to understand and appreciate the *hula*.

Because the language was without written form, memory and a wide variety of long chants were used. This oral literature functioned for Hawaiians very much as Shakespeare or the Bible served English speakers: recitation of genealogies; stories of all kinds; history; songs of joy and awe; prayer; lamentation; and praise of gods, men, and women. As the scholar Adrienne Kaeppler explained:

(Hawai'i's) music was a complex integrated system of poetry, rhythm, melody, and movement that served many functions, from prayer to entertainment. The most important and basic element of this complex was the text. Rendered melodically and rhythmically, the poetry could be interpreted on more than one level ... dance rendered this poetry into visual form by alluding to selected words of the text ... The dancer was essentially a storyteller ... conveying the text depended primarily on movement of the hands and arms.

Hula was an integral part of Hawaiian life as performance art or entertainment; as spontaneous activity for pleasure; as magic in ritual form; and in celebration or honor of people or events. There were casual performers, roving professionals, dedicated students at *hālau hula* (schools) who lived under rigorous religious *kapu*, and dancers who belonged to a chief's court. There were appropriate *hula* for any kind of occasion, from conception and birth to death. Hawaiians dealt with these issues openly, without self-consciousness. *Hula*, Hawai'i's dance of life, barely survived the Western onslaught. The miracle is: it did.

"Iles Sandwich: Femme d'Isle Maui Dansant." A Maui dancer performs a *hula kuhi lima* (seated dance without instruments, emphasizing arm movements). Elaborately tattooed from the waist up, she wears a voluminously draped *pā'ū*. Arago, 1819.

"Danse des Femmes," by Choris, 1816. In the favored short hair of the period and wearing short, intricately draped and tied *pā'ū kapa,* a large group of female dancers entertain Western guests and natives.

"Danse des Hommes," Choris, 1816. In long and short hairstyles, carrying feather-decorated shields, and wearing boar-tusk bracelets and dog-teeth anklets, tattooed male dancers wear short garments similar to the women's. Musicians play large gourd drums and small coconut shell drums. A high-ranking woman in the front row has a *kāhili,* a feather standard.

"*Jeune femme des Iles Sandwich dansant,*" lithograph after Arago. This bare-breasted, seated dancer seems to emerge from voluminous puffs of the *pā'ū* around her hips. She wears a *lei palaoa* of chiefly status, and is missing a tooth. Usually this self-inflicted loss mourned the death of an *ali'i* – quite possibly Kamehameha I, who had died three months earlier.

A presumed ceremonial dance is performed by a single tattooed male with a feather gourd rattle, wearing a *malo* (loincloth), a collar-like necklace, and leg cuffs of dog teeth. Lithograph after Webber sketch, 1778.

"*Scene de Danse aux Iles Sandwich,*" by Lauvergne, 1836, entertainment in Honolulu for the *Bonité*, a French man-of-war. Costumes were Westernized, performers had dwindled, and the dance itself had lost much of its former vitality. Adolph Barrot reported, "Only the singing and the singers appeared to have preserved all the originality of ancient times … (the dancing was) mean and monotonous … far from realizing the idea we had formed of it."

The Hawaiian people were a race of expert fishermen. The art had been handed down from their ancestors … passed on by the grandparents to the boys.
- Samuel Manaiakalani Kamakau,
early Hawaiian scholar

Fishponds on Kaua'i. Kamakau tells us that fishponds "date from very ancient times"; that they beautify the land; that there were freshwater ponds and shore ponds; and that some ponds were as large as 60 to 70 acres, requiring thousands of men to build. Circa 1800, there were about 300 royal fishponds. Built by commoners, they were managed by keepers appointed by the chiefs. Product of the ponds was primarily for chiefs and *kāhuna*.

FISHING IN OLD HAWAI'I: INHERITED SECRETS, CRAFTY RESOURCEFULNESS

Fishing was paramount in the lives of pre-contact Hawaiians. Terrestrial sources of protein were chronically in short supply; and, surprisingly, "the production of marine food resources near the shores of Hawai'i (has) always been limited and liable to depletion." The latter is true because Hawai'i's isolation limited diversity of its marine life; and Island waters were not nutrient rich because of the Islands' position in relationship to currents and quantity of reef habitat.

Fishing, therefore, was needed on a regular and frequent basis. Men fished singly and in groups; and everything about fishing was interwoven with strict rules and ritual. They developed many ways of fishing – catching by hand, spearing, and noosing; with baskets, traps, hooks, and lines; from shore, underwater, and in canoes. The fisherman's life was strenuous and dangerous. His body of

Modern man fishing with an old-style scoop net made from a pliable wood frame.

knowledge is said to have been greater than that of the farmer. He had to memo-rize the undersea terrain both inside and beyond the reef; know currents, weather, the stars, and birds; and, of course, gain in-depth knowledge of each kind of fish. Having to procure canoes and acquire nets and other gear was costly.

Fishermen applied a variety of ingenious techniques and developed great patience in pursuit of fish; they used secrecy and crafty resourcefulness to out-smart fellow fishermen concerning fish habitats and fishing methods. Collective fishing, however – under the direction of a head fisherman – was collaborative. One witness, describing trips in which heavy nets were involved, spoke of 60 canoes, "not fewer than 6000 people, and a catch of 50 or 60 canoe-loads."

Early Hawaiian scholar Samuel Kamakau described a trip to dedicate a new net. Procedures began the day before the trip, with a feast and ritual followed by a *moe kapu*, during which fishermen slept as a group overnight – no one being al-lowed to sleep at home or lie with his wife. Procedure of the trip was highly struc-tured as was distribution of the catch – who received how much, in what order.

All trips began and ended with prayer and ritual. There were fish shrines, gods for fish, and some *heiau* were dedicated to fishing. Prior to 1819, certain kinds of fish were *kapu* to women. Penalty for *kapu* infraction was death.

Torch-fishing with spear and kerosene-fueled torches mirrors the ancient version of the same activity, in which the *lamakū* (torch) was fueled by roasted and shelled *kukui* nuts strung on a coconut frond midrib wrapped in dried *ti* leaves and put in a length of bamboo.

Fisherman in a three-man canoe. Indispensable for food gathering, the canoe alone provided pre-contact Hawaiians access to a critical offshore source of protein. An estimated 6,000-12,000 canoes were in use at the time of Cook, 1779.

Although ancient Hawaiians used several types of fishing net, throw nets are thought to be a 19th-century import by Japanese fishermen. Ancient nets were made of *olonā*, among the strongest of natural fibers.

Spearfishing from shore, along the shallows. In ancient days spearfishing was also done while swimming underwater, as well as by torchlight. Typically spears were made of a hardwood pole, six to seven feet long, with a single sharp point.

CHAPTER 2

MISSIONARIES AND WHALERS

Among the newcomers to Hawai'i were the missionaries, who came not out of curiosity but to bring their concept of the Supreme Being to the natives. It has been said that second only to Cook's accidental arrival, 1778, the most important event in the history of Hawai'i was the arrival of American missionaries, 1820. In November 1819, Liholiho (Kamehameha II) would dismantle the Islands' existing religious system. Calvinist missionaries from New England – having left Boston on the brig *Thaddeus*, October 23, 1819 – would arrive in the Islands April 4, 1820, on a mission of conversion. Their impact was deep and lasting in part because of two early efforts – translating the Bible into Hawaiian, and converting Hawai'i's leaders to their beliefs. Like the Polynesians more than a millennium before them, the missionaries were not content with a passive adaptation; they became involved in all aspects of Hawaiian life, and their influence was felt quickly in religion, customs, morals, even dress.

In America it was a time of great religious zeal. But in 1809 before the missionaries thought of leaving New England in search of souls to save, a young Hawaiian of Kealakekua – the area that had proved fatal for Cook – climbed up the anchor chain of a sailing ship, begging for safety from priests who'd held him captive. Obookiah (*Ōpūkaha'ia*) was a recent orphan of warfare in which both parents and his infant brother had been killed. The captain took him aboard and in New Haven, Connecticut, Obookiah lived with the captain's family. One day the young man was found at Yale College chapel, "weeping because his people were in ignorance." Students tutored him. A bright, diligent and ardent Christian, Obookiah resolved to return to Hawai'i as a missionary. Other young Hawaiians showed up, via the shipping path, and expressed a similar interest. Churches were awakened to an evangelical opportunity. In 1816 they founded a school for the Hawaiians, to prepare them for the ministry, and preaching and teaching in the Islands. Obookiah's early death in 1819 threatened failure for the whole idea. Yet such was the fervor of the New England Calvinists, they transferred the young man's sense of Christian duty to their shoulders, accepting it as their own challenge.

LEFT: A Roman Catholic priest baptizes High Chief Kalanimoku aboard the French corvette *Uranie*, August 1819, about three months after the death of Kamehameha I. Painting by Arago.

Obookiah's dream of Christianizing his home Islands became viable in 1819 when the American Board of Commissioners for Foreign Missions (ABCFM) established the Sandwich Islands Mission. Four days later the new group of volunteer missionaries sailed on the brig *Thaddeus* from Boston, with no expectation of seeing their native land again. A total of 12 companies of missionaries sponsored by the ABCFM went to Hawai'i from 1845 to 1863. These sank deep roots in the soil. Still strong in the 21st century, Christianity has a leadership role in Hawai'i.

Henry Obookiah (Ōpūkaha'ia)

The Reverend Hiram Bingham and his wife, Sybil Moseley Bingham, members of the Pioneer Company of American missionaries, arrived in Honolulu in 1820. Leader of the Mission, Bingham was pastor and designer of Kawaiaha'o Church; played a major role in creating a written form for the Hawaiian language; translated parts of the Bible into Hawaiian; and became a trusted advisor of the king, chiefs, and chiefesses.

Hiram and Sybil Bingham

Carved wooden temple image.

King Kamehameha II (Liholiho, 1797-1824), restless and wanting to see the world, took his wife Kamāmalu to London in 1820.

Queen Kamāmalu (1800-1824). The king's half sister and favorite wife was a flamboyant figure at home and abroad, died in London of measles, July 1824.

High Chief Boki and Chiefess Liliha accompanied Liholiho and Kamāmalu to London, where they proudly wore native dress and sat for this portrait.

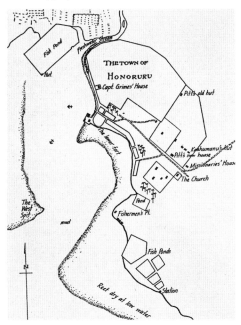

Honolulu map, 1825, by Lt. C. R. Malden, surveying officer on Britain's HMS *Blonde,* on her voyage to return the bodies of Kamehameha II and Queen Kamāmalu. The map records a characteristically Hawaiian element – seven fishponds, thus documenting Islanders' use of aquaculture.

31

One energetic missionary came from England. The Reverend William Ellis was unlike the Americans in other important ways. His writings depicted Hawaiians not as a people in dire need of salvation, but as people of another culture struggling to emerge into modern times. He was sympathetic to the Hawaiians and intensely interested in the way they lived. As a result, he wrote objectively, and about things that other missionaries ignored. His *Narrative of a Tour of Hawai'i, or Owhyhee*, is a remarkable and valuable piece of work. Ellis wrote about Hawaiian hospitality:

> *A transient visitor on arriving among them will generally have an entertainment provided, of which the persons who furnish it seldom partake. The family with which we lodged was, however, induced to join us this evening at supper, though contrary to their ideas of propriety.*
>
> *Whenever we have remarked to the natives that their conduct in this respect is unsocial, they have usually answered, "Would it be right for us to present food to our friends, and then sit down and eat it ourselves?"*
>
> *Connected with this, another custom, equally at variance with our views of hospitality, is practiced by the guests, who invariably carry away all that remains of the entertainment, however abundant it may have been. Hence, whenever a pig, &c. has been dressed for us, and our party have finished their meal, our boys always put the remainder into their baskets and carried it away. To this we often objected: but they usually replied, "It is our custom; and if we don't take it, the people will think you are dissatisfied with what they have provided."*

The beauty of the Hawaiian women was both a blessing and a curse. Venereal diseases, introduced by Cook's crewmen and subsequently the ships that called from all over the world, began the great decline of the Hawaiian population. Cook tried to keep his sailors separated from the Hawaiian women, but it was impossible, as the ship captains who followed Cook also discovered. Between 1820 and 1840—busy years for Pacific whaling—the incidence of diseases among the Hawaiians peaked. The Hawaiians had no natural immunity to diseases that killed them—influenza, mumps, smallpox, whooping cough, scarlet fever, and others. Certainly there was no immunity to the terrible venereal diseases that raced like wildfire through the populace.

Reverend Hiram Bingham took firm charge of the first company of missionaries sent from Boston by the American Board of Commissioners for Foreign Missions. Realizing the

William Ellis

Robert Dampier portraits depicting Liholiho's brother and sister, King Kauikeaouli at the age of 12 and the Princess Nahi'ena'ena. As full siblings and the children of Kamehameha I's sacred wife, Keōpūolani, they outranked their father and under the old order would have married each other. Forbidden by Christianity, and confused and frustrated, Nahi'ena'ena died distraught at 21. Later, Kauikeaouli (Kamehameha III) married Kalama.

A sketch of Hiram Bingham, by himself, preaching at Waimea on O'ahu, 1826. The Queen Regent Ka'ahumanu is present to reinforce Bingham's admonitions.

influence chiefs had on commoners, conversion efforts began with the *ali'i*. The most influential was Ka'ahumanu, who in 1819 had led the way in revolt against religious restrictions of the *kapu* system. Initially, she wasn't anxious to take on the yoke of another set of rules. Patient and persistent, the missionaries were attentive to Ka'ahumanu when she became seriously ill. Gradually she grew attracted to the message of Christ, finally becoming a zealous convert. Just as the missionaries had hoped, she used the full weight of her power, urging others to accept the Christian God.

Soon the huge American whaling industry was attracted to Hawai'i's mid-Pacific location. Supplying the ships that hunted whales and harvested their oil became important to the Islands, especially Maui, where Lahaina flourished as the unofficial whaling capital of the Pacific. Sailors on leave in Hawai'i flocked ashore. Local women also swam out to greet them. Bingham was successful in converting many high-ranking chiefs and chiefesses, and he won their approval to forbid Hawaiian women from visiting the ships. One whaler who fumed at this ruling was the skipper of the *Dolphin*, "Mad Jack" Percival, whose vessel was the first American warship to visit Hawai'i. In 1826, the ship's crew and hangers-on rebelled at a missionary worship service. Bingham described the scene:

> As we were assembling for worship, in and around the house of Kalanimoku, in the afternoon, several seamen, part of whom belonged to the Dolphin, rushed into the spacious hall or saloon in the second story where were Kaahumanu, Kalanimoku, Namahana, and Boki, and a considerable number of others, and with menacing tones and gestures made their demands and threats. "Where are the women? Take off this tabu, and let us have women on board our vessels, or we will pull down your houses. There are 150 of us—the tabu must come off: there is no other way." Thus commenced a riot which occupied the time and place of the expected divine service. These were followed by successive squads. One and another dashed in the windows of Kalanimoku's fine hall, breaking some seventy panes along the veranda. Some, I think, did not intend violence; and one of them said to me, "I wish you to take notice who they are that are doing this; we are not all engaged in it."

The rioting spread to Bingham's house and became more intense before Hawaiians came to the rescue, attacking the sailors. Finally, Lieutenant Percival arrived and calm was restored, but the riot had its intended effect. Bingham continued:

> In the evening of the same day the commander waited on the chiefs and reiterated his objections to the tabu, and, while he admitted that the sailors had gone too far, expressed his unwillingness to leave the country till his vessel should enjoy the privileges that had been enjoyed by the vessels of other nations. Governor Boki and Manuia, the commander of the fort, whose effective agency were then essential to the enforcement of the tabu, yielded to its violation in the harbor of Honolulu.

The whaling men's impact on the Hawaiians was deep and often confusing. The Hawaiians noted the worth of the goods flowing in and out of the ports of Lahaina and Honolulu. They observed the excesses of the whaling men ashore, and all the while their own values crumbled. During this period they lost much of their land and watched as their population dwindled from at least 400,000 down to about 135,000 in 1823. Having lost the *kapu* system that had framed their lives,

An aquatint after Hulsart shows the famous Roach fleet hunting sperm whales off Hawai'i Island, 1833.

Hawaiians were bewildered and hard-pressed to make sense of their lives and time. The missionaries, for all their good intentions and sincere zeal, also brought prejudices and conflicting ideals, so that for a span of time Hawaiians were torn between the whaling men and the missionaries, unable to anchor their beliefs and their spirituality.

Honolulu had grown considerably. In 1823 Williams Ellis described it:

> *Immediately south of the valley of Anuanu (Nu'uanu) is situated the town and harbor of Honoruru; the harbor is the best, and indeed the only secure one at all seasons, in the Sandwich Islands, and is more frequented by foreign vessels than any other; seldom having within it less than three or four, and sometimes upward of thirty, lying at anchor at the same time ... On the eastern side of the basin is a strong fort, one hundred yards square, mounting sixty guns. It was begun by the Russians, who were expelled, but finished by the natives, from an apprehension that these foreigners ... were about to take possession of the island.*

It was a critical time that continued for decades. In regards to *hula*, by about 1840 Charles Wilkes wrote, that dance in Hawai'i had been "interdicted" by missionaries "in order to root out the licentiousness that pervaded the land. They therefore discourage any nocturnal assemblies ... The watchfulness of the government, police, and missionaries is constantly required to enforce the due observance of the laws." The missionaries outlasted the whaling era and ultimately had a deeper impact on Hawai'i than the whalers.

"Diamond Head from Look-out"about 1851, shows the landmark crater later named Punch-bowl. The fort is highlighted at the center, along with the courthouse and Kawaiaha'o Church, completed 1842. Lithograph from Burgess.

Honolulu from offshore in 1848 – showing a mix of Hawaiian and Western ways: both thatch and wood architecture; both canoe and tall ships for transportation.

On a hill above Lahaina, Maui, Reverend Lorrin Andrews founded Lahainaluna Seminary, 1831, for Hawaiians. In early years of the whaling boom, Lahaina Christians – some of them Hawaiian – kept tighter control on liquor than their counterparts in Honolulu. For a while this resulted in fewer whalers calling at Lahaina.

CHAPTER 3

THE HAWAIIAN MONARCHY RULES

Kauikeaouli (Kamehameha III), 1813-1854, reigned for 30 years, the longest of any Hawaiian monarch. During this period, Hawai'i had three forms of government: the controlled regency of Ka'ahumanu; the unpredictable rule of Kauikeaouli, who suddenly had real power; and the constitutional monarchy of kings forced to deal with their increasingly modern world. The *Great Mahele* (system of land division) also marked the reign of Kamehameha III.

After fourteen years as a medical missionary in Honolulu, in 1842 Dr. Gerrit Parmele Judd resigned to serve the Hawaiian government in a variety of influential roles and to pursue business interests. He became secretary of state for foreign affairs, minister of the interior, and commissioner to France, Great Britain, and the United States. Traveling to these countries, 1849-1850, he took two young chiefs educated at the strict missionary-founded Chiefs' Children's School and who both became kings – Prince Alexander Liholiho (Kamehameha IV), and Lot Kamehameha (Kamehameha V).

Kamehameha IV, 1834-1863, and his consort, Queen Emma – out of concern for the health of their subjects – founded The Queen's Hospital. Considered pro-British, they were instrumental in establishing the Anglican Church in Hawai'i. They had an elegant court but experienced tragedy. Their only child, Albert Edward Kauikeaouli, Prince of Hawai'i, died at the age of 4. The King died 15 months later at just 29 years old. As dowager queen, Emma made an unsuccessful bid for the throne following the death of a later king in 1874, but was defeated by Kalākaua.

Lot Kamehameha (Kamehameha V), 1830-1872, succeeded his brother Alexander

ABOVE: Dr. Gerrit Judd.

LEFT: Kauikeaouli (Kamehameha III).

in 1863; adopted a new, less liberal constitution; and worried about the possibility of Hawai'i's annexation by a foreign nation. He proposed to the widowed Emma, was refused, and died a bachelor without naming a successor.

In 1873, William Charles Lunalilo, 1835-1874, became Hawai'i's first elected king. Also deeply concerned with the plight of common people, he founded the Lunalilo Home for aged Hawaiians. One year into his reign he died unmarried and also without naming a successor.

High Chiefess Ruth Keanolani Kanahahoa Ke'elikolani (Princess Ruth), 1826-1883, refused to convert to Christianity, and learned but refused to speak English, leading some to misjudge her considerable intelligence. Her personal life was rife with the tragedy of several deaths. She also missed out on gaining the throne but inherited huge amounts of Kamehameha lands, most of which she left to her cousin Pauahi.

Through these decades Hawai'i was forced to constantly change. The modern world kept intruding with both negative and positive influences. In 1866 a ship stood off Honolulu Harbor, carrying a man who would become known world-wide. Samuel L. Clemens had recently taken on the pen name of Mark Twain, and he was on the threshold of making it ever more famous. In Hawai'i he planned to spend the next four months writing twenty-five articles for the leading newspaper in the American West, the Sacramento *Union*. His first impression:

> *On a certain bright morning the Islands hove in sight, lying low on the lonely sea, and everybody climbed to the upper deck to look. After two thousand miles of watery solitude the vision was a welcome one. As we approached, the imposing promontory of Diamond Head rose up out of the ocean its rugged front softened by the hazy distance, and presently the details of the land began to make themselves manifest: first the line of beach; then the plumed cocoanut trees of the tropics; then cabins of the natives; then the white town of Honolulu, said to contain between twelve and fifteen thousand inhabitants spread over a dead level; with streets from twenty to thirty feet wide, solid and level as a floor, most of them straight as a line and few as crooked as a corkscrew.*
>
> *The further I traveled through the town the better I liked it.*

Hawai'i was beginning to attract people from all over the world, people who came out of curiosity instead of business interests or government necessity. Twain was one of the more famous visitors and among the early better-known writers. A dozen years later another intrepid author—an intense, no-nonsense Yorkshire woman, Isabella Bird—arrived after reporting on other exotic places, including the Vale of Kashmir, the Upper Yangtze, Tibet, and the deserts of Morocco. Miss Bird wrote comprehensively and well. Her book, *The Hawaiian Archipelago: Six Months Among the Palm Groves, Coral Reefs and Volcanoes of the Sandwich Islands*, attracted international interest. Like Twain's works, she helped make the world aware of the far Islands in an azure sea. She may have been the first to voice what became a commonplace term for Hawai'i when she wrote:

> *And beyond the reef and beyond the blue, nestling among coconut trees and bananas, umbrella trees and breadfruits, oranges, mangoes, hibiscus,*

algaroba and passionflowers, almost hidden in the deep, dense greenery, was Honolulu. Bright blossom of a summer sea! Fair Paradise of the Pacific!

Kamehameha IV.

Little Prince Albert.

Queen Emma.

Kamehameha V.

King Lunalilo.

Princess Ruth.

CHAPTER 4

THE REIGN OF KALĀKAUA: CONTROVERSY, MUSIC, MERRIMENT

As an elected sovereign of a constitutional monarchy, who governed as though he believed in the divine right of kings, Kalākaua was easily maligned. He was chosen king by the Hawai'i legislature and took the oath of office in 1874. Extravagant, self-indulgent, and notably unpredictable and capricious – especially about changing ministerial appointments, dismissing Caucasian ministers and replacing them with Hawaiians – his reign was rife with controversy, scandal, and turmoil. Eventually, wealthy sugar businessmen prevailed, forcing him to sign a new constitution the "Bayonet Constitution"). This transferred power to the legislature, severely limiting the King. After long, complicated negotiations, in 1876 Kalākaua accepted the Reciprocity Treaty, giving Hawai'i favorable trade terms on sugar and other items in exchange for U.S. "coaling station rights" at Pearl Harbor. This was celebrated in Hawai'i with "an all night torchlight procession and fireworks."

The Reciprocity Commission: (seated) Governor John Dominis, King David Kalākaua, Governor Kapena; (standing) H. A. Pierce, Luther Severance.

With dreams of an empire – a federation of Pacific Islands with Hawai'i at the helm – in 1887 Kalākaua bought and refitted a trading steamer, commissioned as the *Kaimiloa*. It carried an embassy to Apia, Samoa, but the effort proved to be inept diplomacy, and failed.

Beyond politics and poker games, however, Kalākaua was a scholar, poet, composer of music that lives today, and – above all – a stalwart supporter of Hawai'i's traditional culture and arts,

LEFT: In 1863 King David Kalākaua married Kapi'olani, granddaughter of Kaua'i's last ruling chief Kaumuali'i.

A large crowd at 'Iolani Palace for ancient-style *hula 'ōlapa*, accompanied by chanting and drumming – part of Kalākaua's coronation festivities, February 1883.

particularly the *hula*. Throughout his 17-year reign, Kalākaua steadfastly encouraged the open practice of traditional dance, to the great disapproval of missionaries. It is this legacy that distinguishes him, and for which he is appreciated and honored in the 21st century.

The HMS *Kaimiloa* at anchor, flagship of Kalākaua's ill-fated navy.

Kalākaua surveys his navy, composed in part of boys from the Honolulu Reformatory School.

Lover of life, liquor, and lavish *lū'au*, Kalākaua stands proudly in regal trappings of European monarchial style.

Inspection of Honolulu's police officers at the King Street building housing the police department and district court, about 1885.

Even after the whaling era ended in the 1870s, the malaise in Hawai'i did not. In 1887, King Kalākaua grieved over the condition of his people. In an introduction to Kalākaua's book, *The Legends and Myths of Hawai'i*, R. M. Daggett noted (with the king's approval):

In the midst of evidences of prosperity and advancement it is but too apparent that the natives are steadily decreasing in numbers and gradually losing their hold upon the fair land of their fathers. Within a century they have dwindled from four hundred thousand healthy and happy children of nature, without care and without want, to a little more than a tenth of that number of landless, hopeless victims to the greed and vices of civilization. They are slowly sinking under the restraints and burdens of their surroundings, and will in time succumb to social and political conditions foreign to their natures and poisonous to their blood. Year by year their footprints will grow more dim along the sands of their reef-sheltered shores, and fainter and fainter will come their simple songs from the shadows of the palms, until finally their voices will be heard no more forever.

Queen Kapi'olani, 1834-1899.

In 1881, King Kalākaua was the first monarch in the history of the world to circumnavigate the globe. His wife Kapi'olani stayed home but served as his personal

Charles Reed Bishop, 1822-1915.

High Chiefess Bernice Pauahi Bishop (Princess Pauahi), 1831-1884. She died without issue.

representative in London at Queen Victoria's Jubilee in 1887. Concerned about preserving the Hawaiian race as it continued to decline, Kapi'olani founded a maternity home, now known as Kapi'olani Medical Center for Women and Children.

Other major figures of Kalākaua's era included Charles Reed Bishop, 1822-1915, a native New Yorker and astute businessman. He married High Chiefess Bernice Pauahi, who would twice refuse the throne and inherit the Kamehameha lands from Princess Ruth. Bishop founded Hawai'i's first bank and with his own funds established the Bernice Pauahi Bishop Museum. She founded The Kamehameha Schools/Bishop Estate, becoming Hawai'i's largest benefactor. Her estate totaled approximately 11 percent of Hawai'i's land area. She married but died without issue.

Beloved by his subjects, particularly native Hawaiians, King David Kalākaua remained a thorn in the side of the class of wealthy Caucasian businessmen. His support of *hula* and ancient culture was fiercely criticized in the English-language newspapers as a return to savagery. From the beginning, his reign was burdened by debt and the "Bayonet Constitution" that favored mostly white property owners. His attempts to solve this were controversial, fodder for the English-language newspapers in Honolulu that constantly reported on new scandals. At the age of 54, without issue, Kalākaua died in 1891 of a stroke in San Francisco while on a rest and recuperation trip.

Fire station draped in mourning at Kalākaua's death.

Lei-bedecked Company Two and a decorated fire engine about to join a Jubilee event, November 16, 1886, celebrating King Kalākaua's 50th birthday. Festivities lasted a week and included a parade, regattas, and *lū'au*.

CHAPTER 5

TUMULT: THE END OF THE 19TH CENTURY

In large and small ways, the conflict between two opposing cultures continued all the way to the end of the 19th century. When powerful Queen Ka'ahumanu converted to Christianity and subsequently forbid *hula*, it survived underground, with the exception of periodic court performances. Even then, it was *hula* in missionary-approved costumes designed to conceal a great deal of

Hula dancer in lush *lei maile*, amply covered from neck to knees, including long, puffed sleeves. She is free of leggings and shoes, possibly signifying a later date than 1870s.

what dancers had traditionally revealed. "Dance We Will – No Tabu!" As early as 1821 – just one year after the arrival in Hawai'i of missionaries with their vehement protests against *hula* – Oahu's Governor Boki uttered this defiant outcry against the Reverend Hiram Bingham's admonition against including *hula* in the mourning ceremonies to be held for two *ali'i* on a Sunday. The incident would come to characterize a 50-year conflict between missionary forces doing everything in their power to eradicate traditional values while Hawaiians kept dancing whenever and however they could.

The tide turned with the accession of David Kalākaua, who inaugurated an assertive cultural revival. Following him in 1891, Queen Lili'uokalani was of like mind in cultural matters. Both were musically gifted, missionary-educated, politically controversial Royalists who in their musical responses became bellwethers. While cherishing the Hawaiian language and traditional music and dance, they remained open to new instruments ('*ukulele*, guitar, piano) and new kinds of music (melody and harmony of hymns, brass band).

Actively participating in the blending of these cultural elements, both monarchs served as strong forces in the amalgamation of the traditional and the introduced. This eventually resulted in a form now recognized as "Hawai-

LEFT: Studio photo of *hula*, 1870s. Even before Kalākaua's Jubilee "revival," *hula* was a favorite subject of photographers, striving to capture Hawai'i's exotic appeal with fully clad dancers in front of backdrops.

ian music." The 20th century saw widespread, albeit often superficial, fascination with Hawaiian music and dance. In mid-century, Elvis would rock on stage with his own style of pelvic movement, and for a decade *hula* lost the limelight. In the 1960s, indigenous culture became cool; sex was no longer sinful; and *hula* arose phoenix-like from the hearts of folk who had harbored it all along. In the 21st century, *hula* thrives in a contemporary form and in an evolved traditional form amongst thousands of adherents in Hawai'i, and in a growing body of initiates on the U.S. Mainland, and in Japan and Mexico. However, before all this came about other immense changes in Hawai'i were taking place in the 1890s.

Out of hiding, into public – *hula* at Kalākaua's 50th birthday Jubilee, 1886, where a *hula* dancer was accompanied by *'ukulele*. The audience loved it and the "Merrie Monarch" sanctioned the new music.

Men and women *hula* dancers posed together, 1896, wearing raffia skirts introduced from the Gilbert Islands. Blouses have become more brief.

FATHER DAMIEN: DESOLATION, DESPAIR, HEROISM

It was one of the introduced diseases that proved devastating to Hawaiians – exactly from where or when it came is not recorded. Natives called it *ma'i Pākē* (Chinese disease). Whites identified it as leprosy. In 20th-century Hawai'i it came to be called Hansen's disease, reflecting the name of the man who identified the

bacillus leprae. By any name, it signified dread, disfigurement, and painful death, until the introduction of sulfone drugs in the 1940s.

Hawai'i's Leprosy Act, 1865, provided for segregation of victims, and the village of Kalawao on Moloka'i's Kalaupapa Peninsula was made a settlement site where patients were forcibly sent into lifelong exile. For the following century – until the Board of Health ended the segregation policy in 1969 – more than 7,000 men, women, and children lived out involuntarily confined lives there. Before the Belgian priest Damien de Veuster arrived in 1873, settlement residents were essentially left to survive on their own amid disgraceful, lawless conditions. The more fortunate were accompanied by a *kokua* (helper), usually a spouse or relative. Many, including children, had to fend for themselves. Father Damien voluntarily committed his life to the exiled

Heroic figure – Damien Joseph de Veuster (1840-1889) – canonized in 2009, and now known as Saint Damien.

patients of Kalawao/Kalaupapa, and died among them. Other notable volunteers who dedicated their own lives to aid the outcasts were Brother Joseph Dutton and Mother Marianne Cope.

Damien with female patients, possibly the first Kalaupapa photograph, mid-1870s.

The boys of Baldwin Home, c. 1895, lovingly cared for by Brother Dutton for 44 years.

The Baldwin Home Band by Damien's church, Kalawao. Music was – and remains – an important part of life at the settlement, which moved from Kalawao to Kalaupapa village over a period of several years beginning about 1887.

Baseball – one of many activities organized by Father Damien, Brother Dutton, and Mother Marianne to help patients achieve a sense of normalcy and feelings of accomplishment and joy.

By 1960, the settlement at Kalawao was an organized and tidy community. Today Kalaupapa National Historic Park is still a home and haven for patients who are free to come and go at will.

HAWAIIAN RANCHING: OF CATTLE, HORSES, VAQUEROS AND PANIOLO

The first horses arrived from California aboard the *Lelia Byrd* as a gift for Kamehameha in 1803. Once Hawaiians realized their purpose and potential, they embraced riding with great gusto. In 1830, American, Mexican and Indian cowboys from Baja California arrived to teach Hawaiians how to manage cattle. Hawai'i developed a thriving cattle industry with colorful and hardworking cowboys. Called *paniolo*, the name was derived from the Spanish term for their teachers, *espaniolo*.

A group of women galloping across the plain below Punchbowl Crater, wearing volumi-nous *pā'ū* (skirts) as riding habits. Drawing by A. Plume on the *Galathea*, 1846.

Ranching was new to the Islands – an introduced industry – that became Hawaiianized and very much at home. In fact, cowboy traditions were established in Hawai'i long before they took root in Texas and the American West. With island ranching, the uniqueness of the *paniolo* and their culture stands out. What are the distinguishing features?

To begin, there's the multi-heritage mix of various Polynesian, Western, and Asian backgrounds, which accounts for physical differences and the lilt of voices that carry signatures of different languages. Originally ranching's primary language was Hawaiian, and ranch vocabulary remains well larded with Hawaiian words.

Paniolo built from a base of Hawaiian traditions and values, honed a life-style that incorporates bits and pieces of other represented cultures. Traditionally bareheaded Hawaiians learned that the Spanish-Mexican *vaqueros'* big-brimmed

David Kuloloia, *paniolo*, at 'Ulupalakua on Maui, 1930s. His wide-brimmed, handmade *lauhala* hat and *palaka* (checkered) cloth shirt distinguish him as a Hawaiian cowboy.

sombreros served a highly useful purpose during long days on the range. Taking advantage of already well-developed Hawaiian weaving skills, their love of *lei*, and availability of choice materials, *paniolo* "metamorphosed" the floppy *sombrero* into intricately designed, handwoven *lauhala* (pandanus leaf) hats in various sizes and shapes. These are still worn with hatbands of flowers, feathers, or shells. Reportedly, old-time *paniolo* took special delight in wearing *lei*, especially *maile*, while at work.

Then there is the *paniolo* "talk story" tradition; the *himeni paniolo* (cowboy anthems); and the music played on guitars and *'ukulele* (developed in from the Portuguese *branguiha*, often made of *koa*). Often instruments were tuned *kī hō'alu* (slack key – an old, formerly "secret," way), a seductively sweet Hawaiian technique. But make no mistake, Hawai'i's *paniolo* were and are every bit as rugged,

Roundup in big sky country over Waimea, Hawai'i, at Parker Ranch, 1950s. Its 225,000 acres, 50,000 head of cattle, and 400 working horses made it the largest family-owned ranch in the U.S.

capable, and stalwart as the hard-riding *vaqueros* imported by Kamehameha III to teach the rigorous skills of riding, horse breaking, steer roping, branding, castrating, herding, and moving cattle from shore to ship. A trio of Hawaiian *paniolo* made steer roping history in 1908 when Ikua Purdy won the World's Steer Roping Championship in Cheyenne, Wyoming, while Archie Kaaua took third place and Jack Low sixth place.

The history of Parker Ranch is based on a combination of romantic adventure and efficiency. In 1815, John Palmer Parker, a pioneering, ambitious, and enterprising former New Englander became enthralled with Hawai'i and its people. He made an invaluable business connection with Kamehameha I and wed a granddaughter of the chief. The arrangements worked well for all concerned. Parker's marriage to Kipikane (formalized first by a *kahuna* in traditional Hawaiian ritual and much later in a Christian ceremony) was rock solid. He ran his business operation based on New England industry and Hawaiian cultural mores. Parker learned the language and even became adept at chanting. His interest in and commitment to Hawaiian culture helped form the basis for a ranch *'ohana* (family), notable for loyalty, mutual respect, and admiration. By all reports, Parker Ranch, under John Palmer Parker and Kipikane, established a template for a new lifestyle in Hawai'i, a cultural "marriage" that we recognize still.

Kailua-Kona, 1939. Getting cattle to market in Honolulu from neighbor islands entailed a dangerous process of "swimming" cattle from shore to ship. Introduced by Spanish-Mexican *vaqueros*, after herding the animals to the beach, steers were towed through the surf to a waiting longboat.

Five or six steers were cross-tied to each side of the boat and hauled out through sometimes shark-infested water to a waiting ship, then lifted aboard for the trip to Honolulu. Offshore Kailua-Kona, Hawai'i.

CHAPTER 6

IMMIGRATION, THE FIRST WAVE

Cook's arrival had thrown cultures into conflict. Less than fifty years later there were other white strangers in the Islands, never to depart. They came as sea captains, traders, whaling men, missionaries, entrepreneurs, and often as drifters. They brought new ideas, new ways of thinking, and new and sometimes bewildering behaviors. An 1850 law mandated work for contract laborers and Hawaiians. Refusal could result in "prison at hard labor." As late as 1874 *kanaka maoli* (full-blooded Hawaiians), were prosecuted for *ha'alele hana*, "abandoning work." Fishing and *hula* were more compatible with their culture.

The whaling industry was replaced by sugar plantations in the last quarter of the nineteenth century, which brought workers from China, Japan, the Philippines, and Portugal. The tapestry of the Islands was woven from exotic threads, resulting in a strong and colorful social fabric. Not without its racial incidents and problems, Hawai'i nevertheless developed into a model state for the manner in which different races were able to mix and mingle, to intermarry, and to conduct social and business matters in a spirit of cooperation and harmony. The Islands became, in this respect, the envy of the world.

From Scotland came tenacious and hardworking men. They were hired to work on and manage the sugar plantations that sprang up, and most arrived between 1880 and 1930. They and their descendants would make a lasting impact on the business and social life of the Islands.

Other Europeans came—six hundred Scandinavians beginning in 1881—but most did not stay, preferring other climates and other lifestyles. Some fourteen hundred Germans arrived, as did some Russians, Greeks, and Italians. By 1853 there were some sixteen hundred whites in Hawai'i, but a quarter century later there were almost thirty thousand—20 percent of the population. By the new millennium whites made up close to 25 percent of the Islands' total residents.

From the Atlantic Azore Islands came the Portuguese. In 1878 their migrations began in earnest when the German bark *Priscilla* docked after 116 days at sea, bringing 120 Portuguese contract workers for the sugar plantations. From 1878 to 1913 there were twenty-nine voyages, bringing almost twenty-six thousand people. By 1980 there were at least fifty-five thousand people in Hawai'i of Portuguese ancestry. They brought the instrument that would become the *'ukulele;*

LEFT: Contract laborers recently arrived from Japan, 1889, to augment sugar plantation labor needs. The men on horseback are Caucasian *luna* (field bosses), and were often accused of being overly harsh.

dances like the *chamarita*; and foods such as *malasadas, pão doce,* and *bulo de mel*. Without them, it was said, the Islands would be *uma mesa sem vinho,* a table without wine.

Among the three hundred or so foreigners in Hawai'i at the start of the nineteenth century, was a handful of Chinese. But in 1852 waves of Chinese immigrants, primarily from Guangdong and Fujian, were brought in to work the sugar plantations. They boarded ships to Hawai'i willingly because their own land, torn by the Tai Ping Rebellion, was under the leadership of a mystic who proclaimed himself to be the younger brother of Christ. The entrepreneurial Chinese tended to work out their contracts, then move into the city to open their own businesses. With the Treaty of Reciprocity in 1876, which spurred sugar production by offering tariff advantages to Hawai'i sugar growers, even more Chinese arrived, and began to intermarry. In the new century more than 60 percent had married into another race. Over the course of two hundred years, over forty thousand Chinese came to Hawai'i, making a mark as strong as the brush stroke of calligraphy. They were the first of the Asian immigrants to the Islands, and their accomplishments are legion. Today they make up 5 percent of Hawai'i's population.

The second group of Asian immigrants came from a kingdom famous for its isolation long before it became famous for other things. From the shadow of Mount Fuji the first Japanese immigrant workers arrived in 1868, called the "first-year persons" because they left during the first year of the Meiji Restoration. This had marked the end of the power of the Tokugawa Shoguns and the opening of Japan, closed to foreigners since 1633. The initial group of Japanese laborers found work-related problems too difficult to overcome and returned home. However, in 1885 the ship *City of Tokyo* brought 943 Japanese to Hawai'i as *kanyaku imin,* contract plantation workers. King Kalākaua himself went down to meet the ship.

Men greatly outnumbered women, as most intended to return to Japan with saved earnings following completion of their contracts. Some did; many more sent for families or "picture brides," who came by mail-order arrangement to work in the fields and marry men they knew only from a photograph. Over 60,000 Japanese were living in Hawai'i in 1900.

"Hawaiian Neptune," Keaukaha, Hawai'i. This early 20th-century fisherman, standing by an intercoastal canoe, models traditional attire: *malo* and *'ahu ua* (rain cape made of *ti* leaves).

Steerage aboard the SS *China*, 1901.

As fresh as it gets – live as well as plucked poultry and produce at Sing Mow market on Hotel Street in Honolulu. Proprietor Chun Mow Bew lived upstairs and was joined in business by his sons Soy Sun, Soy Hooh, and Soy Cheong.

Said to be from the Big Island of Hawai'i, this Chinese family represents proud accomplishment as a photographer snaps them before a painted backdrop.

One small boy amid a large multiracial group of women plantation workers, Kīlauea, Kaua'i, 1888. They earned far less than their male counterparts for the same number of hours in the field. Often management kept workers segregated by race in different camps to lessen the likelihood of laborers bonding in opposition to management.

A Portuguese get-together. Typically, early Portuguese families in Hawai'i were large. Church, family, and community defined their character.

Hawai'i's first water buffalo was imported from South China in the 1880s. This buffalo worked a rice paddy with a farmer in McCully, an area adjacent to Waikīkī.

CHAPTER 7

A KINGDOM LOST

In the Hawai'i of pre-Western contact, distinction between classes was extreme, with the *ali'i* class holding the power of life and death over the common people. Change began with the arrival of tall ships from Western nations, became monumental with the abolishment of the *kapu* system in 1819, and continued with the coming of American missionaries. All things Western were superimposed on a nation that was, in large part, open to change. Class distinctions faded – but not completely. Until the end of the 19th century, Hawai'i remained a monarchy with its nobility of *ali'i*. Conditioned for centuries by genealogically determined power, privilege, and prestige, this state of being was the natural order of things for them. It was theirs by birth, the masses serving and paying homage to them. Throughout the profound changes affecting all phases of Hawaiian life, chiefs and chiefesses had a lifestyle distinct unto them and their retainers. Encroaching ideas of democracy notwithstanding, a palpable difference prevailed between *ali'i* and *maka'āinana*, the people of the land.

When the last Hawaiian ruler ascended the throne, the Kingdom was in a chaotic political state. Queen Lili'uokalani was considering a national lottery to boost needed revenue, while Hawai'i's native population was in serious decline due largely to introduced, fatal diseases to which Hawaiians had no immunity.

The "Bayonet Constitution" of 1887, diluting the power of the throne, resulted in resentment among Hawaiians and set in motion a political situation that was precarious by

Two Hawaiian women making *poi*, the nutritious staple derived from the root of the taro plant. Before the *kapu* system was overturned, cooking was a man's job and women were not allowed to eat with men.

LEFT: A cosmopolitan collection of ships characterized Honolulu's bustling harbor in 1892.

This royal outing at John A. Cummins's Waimānalo country house includes three princesses of the Kalākaua dynasty (left to right, seated in chairs): Ka'iulani (age thirteen), Lili'uokalani (heir apparent), and Po'omaikelani (sister of Queen Kapi'olani, Kalākaua's consort).

On February 3, 1889, a *lū'au* at Waikīkī to honor visiting author Robert Louis Stevenson. At the head of the table (left to right, seated): Stevenson; heir apparent Princess Lili'uokalani; King Kalākaua.

Princess Ka'iulani as a child, posing in front of a painted Diamond Head.

Nalani Jones and Princess Elizabeth Kalaniana'ole relaxing at the beach, Koko Head in the background.

Horseback riding in the country – Princess Elizabeth Kahanu Ka'auwai and husband Prince Jonah Kūhiō Kalaniana'ole, late 19th or early 20th century.

the time Lili'uokalani came to the throne at the death of Kalākaua, 1891. Her birth was recorded in semi-secret: "Suddenly, the midwife moved with the *kahuna*… The child was born quickly and the *kahuna* blessed it immediately and almost surreptitiously, for *kāhuna* were not yet welcome where missionaries might appear at any moment." Already the defining cadence of the future queen's life was in play. Opposing elements would be a constant refrain as she struggled to balance Hawaiian *ali'i* traditions with rigid, guilt-focused Christian Congregational mores.

Born Lili'u Kamaka'eha in 1838, to Keohokalole (of chiefly descent) and Kapa'akea (from a line of high chiefly warriors), within hours she was taken as *hānai* (foster) daughter to Konia (high chiefess and granddaughter of Kamehameha the Great) and Pākī. There she spent her first three years embraced by traditions of chiefly rank before being placed – against her will – in the boarding school for chiefs' children under the direction of missionaries who gave her the "Christian" name Lydia Pākī.

Earlier, as was the custom, Konia had composed a name song for the infant *ali'i*, by which she was "given" many blessings of nature – fruits, flowers, rain, the verdant beauties of Nu'uanu Valley. A splendid heritage for a royal princess, and indicative of Hawaiian values and concepts of "ownership" of such wealth – "it could never be hers entirely, for it was shared by all, from 'forest goddesses' to the 'being' of a rainbow *lei* for *pili* grass."

Ultimately, Konia's nonmaterial, spiritual legacy would come full circle in Lili'u's own legacy to the world – the music of her heart. Her music would also be her lifelong joy, her solace, the mitigating resolution to the dissonance that was her destiny. In her words, "To compose was as natural to me as to breathe; … this gift of nature … remains a source of the greatest consolation…"

With her marriage (September 16, 1862) to John Owen Dominis, High Chiefess Lili'u Kamaka'eha became merely Mrs. John Dominis. She signed letters and music "Lili'u Kamaka'eha." When her brother David became king, she became "Princess Kamaka'eha Dominis." It was not until the death of her brother, Leleiohoku, that Kalākaua declared her heir apparent and gave her the name by which the world knows her – "Lili'uokalani." She called it "no name at all."

The Royal Hawaiian Band, founded in 1872 by Kamehameha V, played an important symbolic role in her life. Heinrich Berger, bandmaster, who came to

Hawai'i on loan from Kaiser Wilhelm I, made a name for himself as he turned a ragtag group of undisciplined boys into a highly polished Royal Hawaiian Band. He established a rewarding relationship with Lili'uokalani and, she found someone with whom to share the music of her life.

Following Lili'uokalani's failed attempt to promulgate a new constitution overturning that of 1887, a group of annexationists formed the Committee of Safety. Using armed American sailors in port at the time, they deposed the

John Owen Dominis, Jr. (1832-1891), consort of Lili'uokalani and governor of O'ahu.

Lydia Pākī, about 15. Intelligent, musically gifted, contemplative, and determined, she experienced bouts of unwarranted guilt.

As a young woman High Chiefess Lydia Pākī/Lili'u Kamaka'eha enjoyed swimming, surfing, and moonlight horseback rides; *lū'au*, picnics, and parties, where new *mele* (songs) and chants were part of the fun.

Mrs. John Dominis, 1862.

The *'ukulele* thought to have belonged to Lili'uokalani, and cover sheet of one of hundreds of her compositions.

Heinrich Berger and the Royal Hawaiian Band, c. 1887.

Queen Lili'uokalani (center, seated), members of the royal family, her court, and retainers on a summer outing at the queen's country place at Waipi'o – in 1892, during the most crucial period of her political life.

The Committee of Safety

Queen on January 17, 1893, and formed a provisional government. An annexation committee went to Washington, asking for territorial status within the United States. The committee included: L. A. Thurston, W. C. Wilder, W. R. Castle, J. Marsden, and C. L. Carter.

Lili'uokalani's position was one of perseverance. She continued to look for ways to restore the monarchy. President Grover Cleveland was sympathetic to her and she held him in high esteem. His report to Congress, December 18, 1893, gave her hope. Here are excerpts from his speech:

> ...but for the lawless occupation of Honolulu under false pretexts by the United States forces ... the Queen and her Government would never have yielded to the provisional government ...
> Believing, therefore, that the United States could not ... annex the islands without justly incurring the imputation of acquiring them by unjustifiable methods, I shall not again submit the treaty of annexation to the Senate for its consideration ...
> By an act of war, committed with the participation of a diplomatic representative of the United States and without authority of Congress, the Government of a feeble but friendly and confiding people has been overthrown. A substantial wrong has thus been done which a due regard for our national character as well as the rights of the injured people requires we should endeavor to repair. The provisional government has not assumed a republican or other constitutional form, but has remained a mere executive council or oligarchy, set up without the assent of the people. It has not sought to find a permanent basis of popular support and has given no evidence of an intention to do so. Indeed, the representatives of that government assert that the people of Hawai'i are unfit for popular government and frankly avow that they can be best ruled by arbitrary or despotic power ...

On July 4, 1894, after annexationists created the Republic of Hawai'i from the provisional government, Royalists made a failed attempt to restore the monarchy six months later. The former queen was arrested at her Washington Place home on January 16, 1895 and brought to the renamed Executive Building – her former Palace – where she was escorted in, and confined in quarters on the second floor, awaiting trial. In 1897, a 556-page document signed by over 21,000 Native Hawaiians, "Protest Against Annexation," was presented to the U.S. Congress. Filed away in the Library of Congress, it remained virtually unknown until a scholar discovered the document more than a century later.

"Paul Neumann making his address on behalf of the ex-Queen at her trial in the Palace." Drawing from a photo in the *San Francisco Examiner*, February 16, 1895.

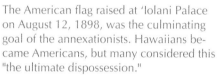

The American flag raised at 'Iolani Palace on August 12, 1898, was the culminating goal of the annexationists. Hawaiians became Americans, but many considered this "the ultimate dispossession."

The United States Navy Bluejackets and marines from the USS *Philadelphia* at annexation ceremonies.

President Sanford Ballard Dole (left) transfers sovereignty of the Republic of Hawai'i to United States Minister Harold M. Sewall (right) as Hawai'i becomes a territory of the United States.

Of the time she was brought to trial, Lili'uokalani later wrote, "My equanimity was never disturbed; and their own report relates that I throughout preserved 'that haughty carriage' which marked me as an 'unusual woman.'"

A poignant moment during ceremonies, April 1982, at the unveiling of Lili'uokalani's statue, when a dancer presents her *ho'okupu* (tribute) with tears in her eyes.

The goal of the annexationists was finally achieved on August 12, 1898, with the transfer of sovereignty, changing the Republic of Hawai'i to the Territory of Hawai'i under United States control. In ceremonies at 'Iolani Palace, "Hawai'i Pono'i," anthem of an independent nation, was played, and the "Star Spangled Banner." For Hawaiians, becoming Americans was "the ultimate dispossession."

LEADERS IN TIMES OF GREAT CHANGE

Despite their noble heritage, the *ali'i* of the late monarchy suffered health problems common to Hawaiians in general of that period. Low birthrate and early death became the norm. By the time Lili'uokalani came to the throne in 1891, following the death of her brother Kalākaua, the monarchy had but one great hope for an heir – Princess Ka'iulani, daughter of Lili'uokalani's sister Princess Likelike and her Scots husband, businessman Archibald Cleghorn. Fate dealt the dynasty a double blow. Lili'uokalani was deposed in 1893; Ka'iulani came home from years of royal grooming in Great Britain and the Continent to find there would be no kingdom for her to rule. She died in 1899, not yet 24.

Miriam Likelike Cleghorn (Princess Likelike), mother of Princess Ka'iulani, died mysteriously at age 37. She is said to have made a deathbed prediction that Ka'iulani would leave Hawai'i for a long time, never marry, and never become queen.

Archibald Scott Cleghorn, native of Edinburgh, Scotland, and a success in the mercantile business, married Chiefess Likelike and fathered Hawai'i's beloved Princess Ka'iulani. An avid horticulturist, he was renowned for his gardens of 'Āinahau in Waikīkī.

At 'Āinahau, the Cleghorn's home (left to right): Prince David Kawānanakoa (Ka'iulani's cousin and possible suitor); Eva Parker (of the ranch family of royal and *haole* genealogy); Rose Cleghorn (half sister to Ka'iulani); and Princess Ka'iulani, back home following eight years of "finishing" in England and on the Continent, 1898.

Victoria Kawekiu Ka'iulani (Princess Ka'iulani), 1875-1899, heir apparent to the Hawaiian throne until the monarchy was overthrown, 1893.

CHAPTER 8

THE AMERICAN TERRITORY OF HAWAI'I

When Queen Lili'uokalani had looked out over Honolulu, she saw a city of contradictions. It was still a sailors' rough port, but had a few paved streets and sidewalks. The *lū'au* torches still burned, but there was gas lighting in some of the buildings. By 1887, 'Iolani Palace itself had gas lighting, before this improvement was made at the White House in Washington, D.C.

The days of barter were gone, for the kingdom now had its own currency, ending the confusion of previous years when myriad coins from many nations were exchanged in Honolulu shops. There was a police force, a fire department, a library, public parks, an ice plant, and a handful of hotels for the ever-increasing visitors. Yet the Hawaiian monarch who was closest to her people had lost her throne. She was made to swear allegiance to a new government and to sign her abdication as queen of Hawai'i. Honolulu became the capital of a U.S. territory in 1898.

After annexation, the Organic Act of 1900 made citizens of all Hawaiians. They became the majority voting bloc—Asian laborers were not eligible—but Caucasians dominated the business and political scenes. Many were conservative Republicans, and some were descendants of the missionary families. The city itself continued to evolve. On several streets, mule-drawn trams made for smooth and easy transportation. Impressive houses of worship flourished.

In the early territorial years, the deposed Lili'uokalani still lived at Washington Place, and nearby was Ali'iōlani Hale, site of the judiciary. Between the former Palace and the

Kawaiaha'o Church was preceded by several thatched versions before being completed in 1842 by Hiram Bingham. It was the scene of royal baptisms, marriages, and funerals.

LEFT: The Seamen's Bethel Church, established 1833 on Honolulu's roiling waterfront, was for sailors and the first church for non-natives. Burned in 1886, its congregation melded into what became Central Union Church.

Our Lady of Peace Catholic Cathedral, completed in 1843, where priests had been expelled earlier, and native believers persecuted. In 1839 the captain of the French frigate *Artémise* demanded religious freedom for Catholics, under the threat of bombarding Honolulu.

In 1862 Kamehameha IV and his wife Queen Emma established O'ahu's first Episcopal church, forming ties with the British monarchy.

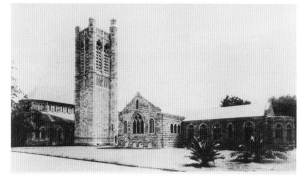

St. Andrew's cathedral took almost a century to complete. It reflects a classic English renaissance style in keeping with Hawai'i's close relationship with Queen Victoria.

harbor, the streets of Honolulu were being wired for telephones, telegraph, and electricity. By April 1901 the Stangenwald Building rose six stories over Merchant Street. There were even a few flush toilets, photo studios, and a skating rink. The first motor cars, both electric, arrived in 1899. A year later an automobile ran two bicyclists off the road at the intersection of King and Kalākaua Streets, likely the first auto accident in Hawai'i.

Prince Jonah Kūhiō Kalaniana'ole and Princess Elizabeth Kahanu Ka'auwai Kalaniana'ole in an early automobile, around the turn of the century. He served as elected delegate to Congress from 1903 until his death, 1922.

The area that had been a yam field belonging to Kamehameha I grew into a business spread encompassing King, Alakea, Beretania, and Nu'uanu Streets. The names reflected the life of the times: Beretania for the British influence. Queen for Kalama, wife of Kamehameha III. Miller Street honored the first British consul general, while Church, Chapel, and Kawaiaha'o Streets were all named for the prominent church. Bethel Street referred to the sailors' chapel, while Alakea (white street) reflected the coral paving of that color.

Leeward was Chinatown, where almost seven thousand people—mostly Chinese—were crammed into fifty acres. In that teeming area in the waning days of 1899 a case of bubonic plague was reported, and the Board of Health decided on a "sanitary burning." Chinatown's citizens were sent to live in quarantined areas on the outskirts of town. On January 20, 1900, a fire deliberately set near Beretania Street and Nu'uanu Avenue was wind-whipped across rooftops and out of the reach of firemen. People in Honolulu fled in panic. A column of dense black smoke rose over the city, and smaller fires sprang up. Before it was brought under control, the fire destroyed thirty-eight acres of Chinatown, a devastating blow to a great number of residents. Thousands were forced to live in quarantine camps, and claims against the government were not settled for months. The ousted residents of the area claimed the fire had been allowed to spread to give the Caucasians more room to expand businesses downtown.

The Great Chinatown Fire in Honolulu was one of the seminal events of the early twentieth century. It was followed shortly by a profound event—as World War I ensued, Hawai'i had to look hard at its mid-Pacific location and begin to think in geopolitical terms.

A purging of the plague, December 1899. Following confiscation of their personal effects, and antiseptic baths, these men received new clothes and were sent to quarantine camp at the Kaka'ako Rifle Range.

Downtown Honolulu during the Chinatown fire, January 20, 1900.

The "sanitary burning" got out of control and spread into other parts of Honolulu, 1900.

38 acres of Chinatown were burned and caused deastating losses, 1900.

CHAPTER 9

SOLDIERS AND A SHIFTING POPULATION

The 1914 outbreak of World War I in distant Europe had a depressing effect in Hawai'i. The Islands became fevered with anti-German sentiment, to the point that schools demanded a loyalty oath, and persons with German-sounding names were inspired to change them or hide them. German language courses were dropped from school curricula. There were some unwarranted persecutions, and for many Islanders the end of the war could not come soon enough. Adding to the tensions, the American military flooded into Hawai'i. Fort Shafter became an important army complex, and Schofield Barracks grew to be the largest army outpost in the world. More and more ships were in the sea lanes in and around Pearl Harbor. Civilian-military tensions smoldered, occasionally flaring into criminal acts on one side or the other.

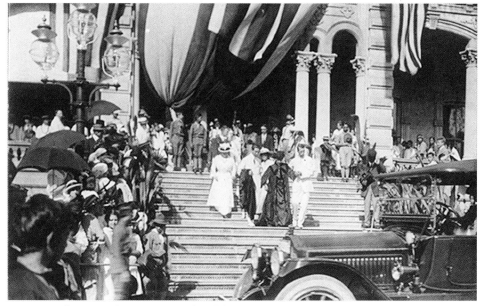

In 1916, still *mō'i wahine* (queen) to her followers, Lili'u emerges from her former palace, the only time she entered it after being imprisoned there following the overthrow.

LEFT: Two Chinese beauties with an American flag as a backdrop, perhaps symbolizing dual pride, 1914.

83

Former Queen Lili'uokalani at end-of-year exercises, 1914, St. Andrew's Priory, a private school for girls. She founded Queen Lili'uokalani's Children's Center on behalf of neglected children.

Indomitable Lili'uokalani in 1914, 21 years after being deposed she appeared with Sanford B. Dole (left) who had been instrumental in her overthrow. At right, then-Governor Lucius E. Pinkham. The occasion, to boost patriotism, had been arranged by the queen's longtime friend the bandmaster Heinrich or Henry Berger (standing).

Mele Kaupoko, a symbol of cultural struggle, wearing a somber all-covering, missionary-imposed garment while the *lei palaoa* around her neck and the feather *kāhili* in her hand proclaim chiefly status.

Old-style native cooking – no deep-frying and no women in the "kitchen." Men cooked (pig, fish, chicken, dog, bananas, sweet potatoes, yams, taro, and breadfruit), steaming food long and slowly in an *imu* (underground oven) with hot rocks.

Charles Kauha (by J. A. Gilman, Jr.) shows two native habits sternly discouraged by missionaries – "wasting" time at the beach surfing and wearing almost no clothes.

"Native Taro Vender," in Western garb, carries a load of the indigenous, labor-intensive crop, taro – both root and tops nutritious.

Indigenous architecture, imported livestock. The preferred thatching material for "grass houses" was *pili* grass. Over the doorway it remained untrimmed until the house was ready to occupy. Then a ceremonial cutting of the *piko* (navel cord) of the house was performed and the thatch cut.

In seven languages, this World War I poster hawks U.S. government war savings stamps.

Men of the Makiki fire station knitting scarves for American soldiers on the European battlefields, 1918.

Big crowds and the Stars and Stripes galore in downtown Honolulu. American patriotism on parade during World War I, with a Pearl Harbor group in the foreground.

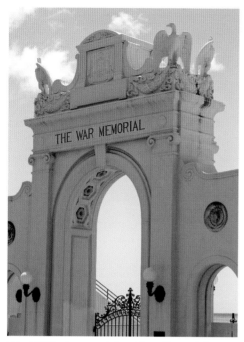

World War I memorial to Hawaiian soldiers who died in Europe.

The Executive Building, formerly 'Iolani Palace, festively lit and arrayed in bunting to honor the United States Navy fleet, 1925.

By 1918 tensions in Honolulu simmered down to an uneasy truce. Civilians recognized the economic impact of federal dollars, while the military grew to appreciate Hawai'i as an outpost. Inevitably, the old trade of prostitution flourished along with dozens of new military-connected businesses, and the trade continued in Hawai'i long after the end of World War I. Meanwhile, some in both the military and civilian camps came to recognize that the two communities could live in harmony if they understood each other a little better, and efforts were made—particularly by the Chamber of Commerce of Hawai'i—to mend fences. Military expenditures were growing to become a vital part of the economy, and would remain so, and the young servicemen and the local people were learning to tolerate each other. Nobody, at the time, had any idea that in the near future there would be a repetition of the military "invasion" of Hawai'i on an even grander scale, and that the reason for it would begin with a shattering surprise attack on military bases in the Islands.

In the years following World War I the Japanese in Hawai'i saw America, fearful of too much foreign labor, close its door to Asian citizenship and Asian immigration. Japanese males were not much inclined to intermarry anyway, and the years 1908-1920 became the era of the "picture brides," young Japanese women brought on contract to Hawai'i to marry Japanese men. The Japanese population increased so that by 1920 more than 40 percent of Hawai'i's population was Japanese. In a century, Hawai'i's Japanese population climbed to more than a quarter of a million. Individual Japanese rose to positions of power, becoming prominent in politics, labor unions, and government. In time the first non-Caucasian governor of Hawai'i would be an American of Japanese ancestry. By the early 1990s in Hawai'i, people of Japanese ancestry represented nearly 25 percent of the population.

Formal *kimono* and the young woman in traditional Japanese headdress are probably for a wedding photograph. Hairstyles of the two standing young women suggest a 1920s time frame.

A young Korean family posed on a Hawaiian *lauhala* floor mat. The father moved ahead in a thoroughly modern American suit; the mother maintained tradition in decorous Korean dress.

Other immigrants from Asia also came across the Pacific. In 1882 America was the first Western country to make a treaty with an ancient land of tough and energetic people, a place called The Land of the Morning Freshness. Korea was suffering political unrest, and its emperor saw greater opportunities for his people in Hawai'i. In January of 1903, about one hundred Koreans arrived in Hawai'i to seek their destinies. They looked beyond the plantations for opportunities; within three years there were more than forty-five hundred Koreans in Hawai'i, noted for their high degree of literacy and their willingness to intermarry. In the second half of the twentieth century they became one of the larger immigrant groups, all upwardly mobile, highly adaptable, and retaining their inherent energy and strong will.

Filipinos came to Hawai'i with musical languages and a propensity for hard work. Their immigration began in 1906, and like others they came because of unrest in their own country and opportunities in Hawai'i. The Spanish-American

War had just ended, and the U.S. was in charge of the Philippines. There seemed no reason why Filipino laborers could not be recruited for plantations in the Islands. Despite poor pay and working conditions, by 1930 there were more than sixty thousand Filipinos in Hawai'i. Some went on to the U.S. Mainland, some returned to the Philippines, but many stayed.

The sleeves and hats tell the story: the lovely ladies celebrate the culture of the Philippines.

CHAPTER 10

WAIKĪKĪ AND SURFING

Nature's abundant blessings positioned Waikīkī to be a chosen place. Early chiefs of O'ahu chose Waikīkī as their seat of power because it offered the best of land and sea: a wide reef-protected bay and beach for their canoes; accessible fishing grounds; freshwater streams feeding rich wetlands advantageous to agriculture and aquaculture; and, for pleasure, cooling trade winds and fine waters for surfing and swimming. Lacking beasts of burden and the wheel in pre-Western contact Hawai'i, travel anywhere was either by foot or canoe. Transportation of goods and materials was a manual matter. This made people of all classes equally adapted to hard work and athletic sports. Many early accounts by travelers cite strong swimming and surfing skills among Hawaiian men and women.

Surfing, F. Howard, 1824.

When Kamehameha the Great conquered O'ahu in 1795, he chose Waikīkī to establish his court. Later on the same site, the Royal Hawaiian Hotel would rise as center of the modern resort area. In time, the warrior-king acquired Western vessels, requiring a deeper harbor than Waikīkī provided. He then moved his court westward to the port of Honolulu, keeping a compound in Waikīkī for purposes of pleasure. The cool breezes afforded a respite from the dry, dusty plains of Honolulu. Kamehameha is said to have enjoyed surfing at Waikīkī, along with his wife Ka'ahumanu and their retainers.

Was this the first use of Waikīkī as a resort? It may have marked the beginning of a concept about Waikīkī that remains essentially unchallenged two centuries later – a great place to go for rest and renewal. Many 19th-century chiefs and chiefesses after Kamehameha had principal residences in central Honolulu, augmented by beach houses at Waikīkī, where relaxed informality prevailed over the more formal city protocol. Among the *ali'i* who acquired homes in Waikīkī for retreat and casual living were: Kamehameha IV;

LEFT: By the 1920s, riding the waves at Waikīkī, with the famous profile of Diamond Head in the background, became a fantasy for many Americans.

Kamehameha V; King Lunalilo (who willed his to Queen Emma); Princess Bernice
Pauahi Bishop; King Kalākaua with Queen Kapi'olani; and Queen Lili'uokalani.
Archibald Cleghorn, the Scots businessman who married Princess Likelike and
became the father of Ka'iulani, last heir to the throne, had a large Waikīkī estate
where he built the fabled 'Āinahau. Sometimes in the evenings, the ill-fated Princess Ka'iulani and friends would go for a cool "bath" in their nightgowns in the
waters of Waikīkī.

A pastoral Waikīkī, c. 1880, in the foreground
that isle insignia – a line of coconut palms.
One coconut grove in Waikīkī was said to
have had 10,000 trees.

Two men with fishing canoes at Waikīkī
Beach, c. 1890.

Waikīkī Beach stretched out in panorama during halcyon days, as it blossomed into a popular
resort for well-to-do travelers after the opening of the five-story Moana Hotel, 1901.

Decorous beach attire for women, c. 1905.

Reflecting the spirit of the times, in about 1930 a group of visitors enjoys the beach.

Beach scene, c. 1946 – postwar exuberance prevails: World War II is over; the Japanese are defeated; the "swimsuit police" are defeated; and the navy is out to do reconnaissance duty.

By 1913, some women swimmers were ready to break ranks by wearing more practical garb – boys' swimming suits – a practice the mayor railed against, proposing a law forbidding it. However, progress continued. Between World War I and World War II, Mainlanders displayed a joyful, playful innocence as they embraced superficial Hollywood/Tin Pan Alley/vaudeville versions of Hawaiiana. Authentic it wasn't; but the world loved it, and Hawai'i became the fantasy of millions.

The sport of surfing captured the world's imagination, and from the beginning was associated with one man. Duke Kahanamoku brought international recognition to the Islands with Olympic medals in 1912, 1920, 1924, and 1928. He spent most of his life living in Waikīkī, in the role of consummate waterman and ambassador of *aloha*. As a swimming and surfing legend, "The Duke's" position in the history of world-class athletes was recognized in 2002, with a U.S. postage stamp bearing his image.

Waikīkī's "beach boys" also became famous and the favorites of visitors to the elite hotels. Noted not only for surfing, canoeing, lifesaving, swimming and teaching abilities, they were also expected to play the *'ukulele* and sing. Big boards were the norm, as were colorful names.

Visitors were fascinated by tandem surfing, and eager to try it. The long low waves at Waikīkī guaranteed a steady, thrilling ride to shore. "Lucky you come Hawai'i," locals said to visitors. To tandem surfers they said, "Lucky you come Hawai'i *now*, not *then*." In ancient times surfing was not only the "sport of kings," certain surfing sites were *kapu*, reserved exclusively for chiefs and chiefesses. And forget about tandem surfing anywhere if you were not of the *ali'i* class. The penalty for that *kapu* violation was death.

By the mid 1930s, large flying boats crossed the Pacific in connection with Pan American's exploratory flights. They were symbolic of things to come, traveling along Waikīkī's miracle mile as they approached Hawai'i. After World War II wide-bodied jets took this same route and turned the famous beach into a Mecca for the masses.

Aerial view of Waikīkī about 1930. The Royal Hawaiian Hotel stands in isolated splendor on the site where Kamehameha I established his court after conquering O'ahu.

Duke Paoa Kahanamoku, 1890-1968, with his *koa* and redwood board, c. 1930s.

The Famous Sikorsky 42 – first of the large flying boats to cross the Pacific, April 1935.

Tandem surfing, with Diamond Head in the background.

Seven of Hawai'i's acclaimed beach boys (left to right): Charles Soupy Coelho; Blue Makua; Turkey Love; David P. Kahanamoku, the beach boys' captain; Ox Keaulani; Curly Cornwell; and Louis Kahanamoku.

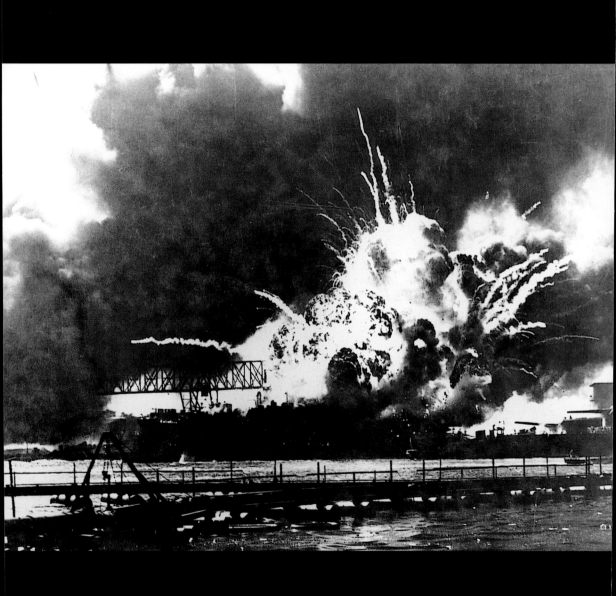

CHAPTER 11

WORLD WAR II

On a calm day in December 7, 1941, the Japanese Empire struck Hawaiʻi with complete surprise, having sent a task force of thirty-one ships undetected across the North Pacific. From four aircraft carriers, the first of 360 aircraft crossed the northern coast of Oʻahu at 7:55 a.m. and began a devastating attack. A second wave followed, aimed at military bases across the Island. When the attack was completed, 21 ships in Pearl Harbor were sunk or heavily damaged, 92 navy planes were lost and 31 damaged, and the army air corps lost 96 and had 128 damaged. The attacking force lost 55 airplanes and 5 midget submarines. While 64 Japanese were killed and 1 captured, 2,390 Americans were killed and 1,178 were wounded.

Among the dead on Oʻahu were 49 civilians, many of them killed by American shells that fell short of attacking aircraft. It was Hawaiʻi's first taste of World War II, but it was by no means the last. On the very day of the attack, military censors went to work. Restrictions were put on newspapers, magazines, and radio broadcasts. In a matter of hours, the military declared martial law throughout the Islands, and Lieutenant General Walter Short declared himself the "military governor" of Hawaiʻi. Both mail and long-distance telephone calls were subject to censorship. All calls had to be in English so an eavesdropping censor could understand all that was being said. Callers could not discuss the weather, among other topics. Long lines for some goods became commonplace. Because of gas rationing, buses were crowded with servicemen jostling civilians for space. Liquor also was rationed. Fresh eggs were hard to come by, as was meat. Home victory gardens sprouted, one estimate putting them at fifteen thousand by August 1942, and thirteen community gardens were cultivated in parks and vacant lots.

Labor shortages became acute with men away in service. Women filled many jobs, including some they had been denied, such as driving trucks and other heavy equipment, and even repairing them. Some became welders, while others worked at aircraft maintenance.

Trenches and shelters were constructed throughout Oʻahu, and air-raid drills were held. There seemed to be little doubt that the Japanese would attack again, but as the months went by the skies over Hawaiʻi remained clear, except for a two-aircraft Japanese reconnaissance flight on March 4, 1942. The flight ran into

LEFT: The ammunition magazine of the USS *Shaw* explodes, cutting the ship in half. The near half would stay afloat and later be reconstructed.

heavy cloud cover, and one aircraft dropped its bombs out to sea while the other dropped them on an undeveloped area of Tantalus, a hilly area above Honolulu.

In the city, some buildings were painted in camouflage colors. The Honolulu Academy of Arts and the Bishop Museum moved valuable works to safer places. Soldiers and sailors—and civilian helpers—strung barbed wire on vulnerable beaches. Honolulu was divided into two evacuation zones by the Office of Civil Defense, and instructions were issued concerning what to carry if one had to evacuate. Women and children were to be the evacuees, while males over fifteen years of age were to stay to fight fires. The military took over half the public parks on O'ahu for storage sites; schools were seized; and sugar and pineapple plantations gave up land, equipment, and men. One historian notes that more than three hundred thousand acres of land were occupied by the military in Hawai'i during the war years. Curfew and blackouts were enforced vigorously, and everyone over the age of six had to be fingerprinted and carry an identification card.

The battleship USS *Arizona* burns furiously after sustaining a direct hit, exploding ammunition – 1,177 sailors and marines perish.

Ford Island – from a camera on a Japanese plane as it makes a diving attack toward Battleship Row, Pearl Harbor, December 7, 1941.

On Ford Island, crewmen watch the devastation around them and along Battleship Row.

For the Japanese in the Islands, it certainly would never be the same. At first denied the opportunity to serve, young Japanese males did whatever they could for the war effort until the military finally allowed them to volunteer. Some were already in the Hawai'i National Guard, and when they were forced out due to their race, some formed the Varsity Victory Volunteers. They eventually segued into units, the 100th Battalion and the 442nd Regimental Combat Team. In the spring of 1943, 2,686 Hawai'i volunteers, Americans of Japanese Ancestry (AJAs) formed the 442nd Infantry Regimental Combat Team. As a segregated unit they went on to win glory and suffer high casualty rates in Europe. The 442nd distinguished themselves in Italy and France, becoming the most decorated unit – for its size – in American history. Over half a century later one of its surviving members, Edward M. Yamasaki, wrote: "I believe (their) major contribution lies in their having helped make America a better, richer place in which to live for everyone; we have seen appreciable increase in sensitivity to the rights of all its citizens, including minorities, and in offering of equal opportunities in education, the arts, politics and business."

442nd Infantry Regimental Combat Team in 1943 gathered at 'Iolani Palace in a historic send-off.

It was the Japanese way of proving a point. One family's experiences show the complicated nature of racial and national prejudice at the time. As of December 7, 1941 the Otanis were among 160,000 Japanese in Hawai'i (37 percent of the population, compared to 25 percent Caucasian). Their Mānoa Valley home had been purchased a year before against objections by Caucasian neighbors. The evening of the attack, the family's father, Matsujiro, was seized and incarcerated as a Japanese enemy alien for the duration of the war. The mother Kane would send four of five sons off to military service. One son, Jay, remained to operate the family business importing food for military and civilian use, working for the Honolulu Police Department as a curfew warden, and also undercover – even from his family – for military intelligence.

After the war Hawai'i's Japanese citizens continued to prove their loyalty and value to America—the veterans went to college on the G.I. Bill and returned to the Islands to move swiftly and decisively into powerful political posi-

The Matsujiro Otani family in 1943: matriarch Kane Otani; eldest son Jiroichi; his wife, Elsie; and son Kenji. Absent is patriarch Matsujiro. The photo commemorates Kenji's departure to serve in the U.S. Army.

tions. Never again did anyone question their patriotism or their rights to whatever political, economic, or social positions to which they would aspire.

Following the Pearl Harbor attack, volunteer civilian women engaged in vital, top secret work for the U.S. Army. "The least known of the women's uniformed services," the Women's Air Raid Defense (WARD) had the "responsibility of plotting and evaluating radar reports on all air and surface craft for the Hawaiian Islands area" throughout World War II. They numbered in the hundreds, in units on various islands. Not even their families knew the nature of their assignment or even where they worked. Recruited primarily from Island residents, when demand exceeded available supply, some recruiting was done – with great secrecy – on the mainland United States.

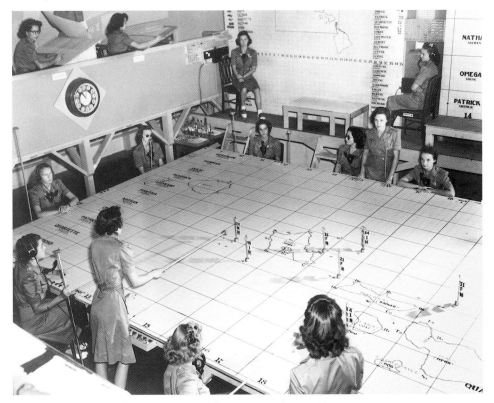

Women's Air Raid Defense group at work on a map of Hawai'i.

The young American men who came to Hawai'i during the war years were as varied as the nation they came from, and military-civilian liaisons took place in places ranging from houses of prostitution to the homes of wealthy and influential Islanders. The war lent an urgency to romances. Many men stationed briefly in Hawai'i went on into the Pacific, some never to return. It was a time when hearts were broken in the bittersweet atmosphere of the conflict and the Islands. It was clear that Hawai'i would never be quite the same.

Marital law lasted far longer than it should have. In 1942 the territory's governor, Ingram Stainback, and its attorney general, J. Garner Anthony, went to Washington to ask the secretary of the interior, Harold Ickes, for help. Through

Sailors get a *hula* lesson from the beloved comedienne, "Hilo Hattie." Clara Melekahaili Nelson taught school for 20 years before entertaining audiences in Hawai'i and on the Mainland, with such comic numbers as "The Cockeyed Mayor of Kaunakakai" and "When Hilo Hattie Does the Hilo Hop."

Military activity extended to Maui, where Frankie and Johnnie's Lunch Counter and shoe shine boys attracted off-duty soldiers and sailors.

Ickes's influence many restrictions were eased, but it was not until October 24, 1944, that President Franklin D. Roosevelt abolished martial law in the Islands. Hawai'i residents could breathe easier, freed from many annoying and often unnecessary restrictions.

Finally, after four days of high-intensity expectation and false reports – including a two-hour celebration on August 12 – official confirmation of victory arrived at 1:42 p.m., August 14, 1945. In Hawai'i, jubilant pandemonium followed. The city celebrated for two days and, again on September 2 – the official V-J Day when the Japanese formally surrendered aboard the SS *Missouri* in Tokyo Bay – with the Honolulu Victory Parade. The city erupted with relief.

V-J Day in Honolulu, with crowds of servicemen.   Civilians celebrated from a balcony.

The good news was accompanied by somber reflection.

CHAPTER 12

SUGARCANE AND PINEAPPLE

Already in the Islands when Captain Cook arrived, *kō* (sugarcane) eventually played a major role in the history of Hawai'i. For over 150 years sugar was the main industry. Importing labor from numerous nations – east and west – established a basis for Hawai'i's famous multiracial society. Control of sugar production was a major factor in political complexities leading to the overthrow of the monarchy and subsequent annexation to the United States.

Ancient Hawaiians had a sophisticated system of agriculture and foreigners were eager to exploit the land and water for sugarcane cultivation. In the 1850s, throughout the world sugar was rare and expensive. The number of plantations in Hawai'i grew from seven to 63 in 1890, with 224,000 acres under cultivation by 1974.

Work in the cane fields required care and protective clothing from razor-sharp leaves.

This vegetable farmer takes her offering of fresh produce directly to cane workers at the Waimānalo plantation, O'ahu.

For over a century, sugar was in such demand that huge fortunes were made and attracted foreign investors. Growing, harvesting, milling and transporting for refinement in the continental U.S. consumed the energy of generations on six major islands. Sugar also made the "Big Five" companies in Hawai'i wealthy. During World War II, sugar was so important that the Islands' entire crop went to the U.S. military. Scientific research improved methods of production into the 1980s, when plantations declined due to changes in the world market.

The exotic pineapple, long a symbol of hospitality, was introduced in Hawai'i by Don Marin in 1813. The Islands' climate and rich soil made the Hawai'i/pineapple "marriage" a perfect match; but learning how to successfully grow the fruit, and to harvest, preserve, and market it, took the rest of the 19th century. The industry began to take off at the beginning of the 20th century. In 1903, Hawaiian Pineapple Company's first total, at Wahiawā cannery on central O'ahu, netted 1,893 cases. Their Iwilei cannery's first total in 1907 netted 2,250,000 cans.

By 1920, O'ahu, Moloka'i, Maui, and Kaua'i had pineapple plantations. Canned pineapple was the territory's second industry, accounting for almost all of the world's output. By 1929, James Dole's Hawaiian Pineapple Company had turned Lāna'i into one big plantation, and his Iwilei cannery in Honolulu was the world's largest. For half a century or more, during the summer peak of the canning season, Island students by the hundreds found employment at the cannery, a job many later recalled as noisy, grueling work. Lines of neatly uniformed packers carefully inspected and graded pineapple slices, then placed them in the appropriate cans. Gloves, workers reported, did not protect their hands from the sticky, irritating juice.

Narrow gauge trains, often with portable tracks, brought harvested cane to sugar mills.

Raw sugar bagged for shipment to sugar refineries in California.

After World War II there was another surge of immigration, as more than seven thousand Filipinos made the journey to the Islands. The Filipinos are credited with the success of the pineapple and sugar plantations, but they did not confine themselves to the production of agriculture. As years passed the Filipinos began to have a more profound impact on the political and social events taking place in Hawai'i.

With a background of the steep Ko'olau range, acres of pineapple fields define central O'ahu's landscape.

Before mechanization supplanted manual labor (c. 1930s), field hands picked the prickly fruit and carried it in shoulder slings to the nearest field road to be picked up.

Amidst the clatter of machinery, workers put sliced pineapple in cans.

Pineapple packing at the plant on Honolulu's waterfront, ca. 1950s.

Boxed cans of pineapple prepared for shipment world-wide.

CHAPTER 13

FROM 1945 TO STATEHOOD IN 1959

The end of World War II was like the opening of a door onto a new era. The veterans of the 100th Battalion, the 442nd Regimental Combat Team, and the other units in which Americans of Japanese ancestry had served so well, were inclined to change the political posture of the Islands. In 1954, they did. That was the year of the great political revolution that saw most of the old Republican power elite turned out of office as a new Democratic party power elite moved in.

The new focus gave rise to a concomitant demand for statehood, as more and more people demanded greater representation. Territorial status suddenly was not enough. The governor of Hawai'i was not an elected official, chosen by the people of the Islands, but a political appointee. Islanders could send a delegate to Congress, but the delegate could not vote. The U.S. Congress retained the power to establish or abolish legislative positions in Hawai'i and could, if it wished, even abolish the territorial government. The implication was that the people of the Islands were not capable of making their own informed decisions. There was, as well, a strong hint of racism, with some southern congressmen looking askance at Hawai'i's brown and mixed races.

For the governing establishment in Hawai'i, change meant a certain amount of risk. They were joined in apprehension by some Hawaiians and by some of the old *kama'āina* (native) elite, whose memories were, perhaps, of a more gracious time. Still, most Islanders favored statehood, as did the territorial legislature and the media. The labor unions came in for a great deal of scrutiny, particularly the International Longshoremen's and Ware-

Two of Hawai'i's biggest boosters: the Islands' celebrated Olympic swimming champion, Duke Kahanamoku, and 50s radio and television star Arthur Godfrey, who contributed to a revival of interest in the *'ukulele*.

LEFT: At a time when America had only 48 states, the Hawai'i Statehood Commission and the Hawai'i Visitors Bureau entered this float in the 1949 Inaugural Parade in Washington, D.C.

Three laborers at work on an irrigation ditch, 'Ewa Plantation, O'ahu.

Philip P. Maxwell (left), Employers Council president, with labor leader Jack Hall (right), 1964, 20th anniversary year of Hawai'i sugar workers.

On February 10, 1954, in a daylong rally on Bishop Street in Honolulu 116,000 Hawai'i residents signed the "Statehood Honor Roll" petitioning Congress for statehood. The effort achieved publicity but not statehood.

housemen's Union (ILWU). The ILWU was the largest, most controversial, best-led, and most militant union in Hawai'i, and was often accused of harboring Communists. Its charismatic leader was Jack Wayne Hall, a brilliant, hard-drinking, hardworking, and pragmatic man. The unions, and especially the ILWU, became a force in Island life, and they were often an irritant to businessmen and politicians.

The specter of Communism began to fade from the unions at the same time as the thrust for statehood was rising. One of the factors that brought about greater acceptance of the unions was that many members of the ILWU had joined other Hawai'i men in going off to Korea to fight the Communists. Meanwhile, Hawai'i's strategy shifted from coupling Alaska and Hawai'i statehood concerns to allowing Alaska to become a state first; the rationale was that once Congress accepted Alaska it could not then deny Hawai'i. This proved to be true. In May 1958 the Alaska statehood bill passed the House, and in June it passed the Senate. Alaska became the forty-ninth state, and Hawai'i began its all-out push for statehood.

Statehood strategies continued, with this well-planned photo of the statehood delegation prepared to leave for Washington. (Left to right) Hawai'i Chief Justice E. A. Towse; Hawai'i Senate President Wilfred C. Tsukiyama; Hawai'i Governor Samuel Wilder King; U.S. Congressman Hiram L. Fong.

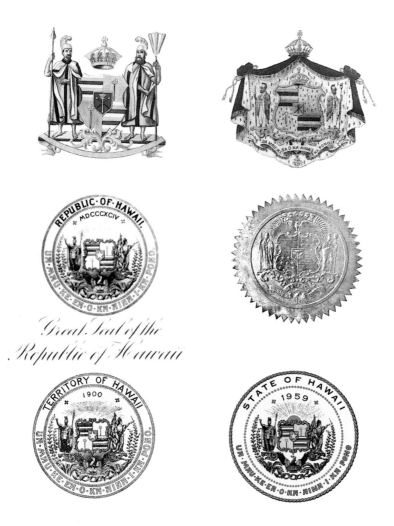

Hawai'i's coat of arms had its beginnings in 1842, when Kamehameha III sent representatives abroad to negotiate treaties to guarantee Hawai'i's continued independence and, further, to ask professionals about design of a royal seal or crest. The first version was prepared by Herald's College, London. The version adopted in 1845 served with little modification throughout the monarchy and remains the basis for the statehood seal. (Left to right, top row) Coat of Arms, Hawaiian monarchy, London, 1843-1844; Coat of Arms, 1883 (King Kalākaua's coronation invitation); (Left to right, middle row) Great Seal, Republic of Hawai'i, 1893; Transitional Seal, provisional government, 1896; (Left to right, bottom row) Territorial Seal, 1900; Coat of Arms, State of Hawai'i, 1959.

In February 1959 the House Committee on Interior and Insular Affairs voted favorably for Hawai'i statehood, and the Senate followed suit in March. On March 11, 1959, the Senate passed the statehood bill, and the next morning the full House of Representatives also passed it. On March 12 there was an air of expectancy in Hawai'i. Then the news flashed that Hawai'i was—at long last—the fiftieth state.

Church bells began to peal all over the city. People poured out of buildings and into the streets to greet one another as fully represented United States citizens.

President Eisenhower designated August 21 as Admission Day, and in Honolulu the Royal Hawaiian Band marked the occasion at 'Iolani Palace, once again the coming-together site for a historic status-changing event.

Civil defense sirens sounded. Newspapers began preparing extra editions. That night there were bonfires on the beaches that had known the footprints of the old Polynesian voyagers. Some groups gathered in churches to hear ministers invoke God's blessings on this newest state. Bartenders were busy, which meant police were busy trying to see that people were not hurt. There was a general mood of euphoria.

But not for all. Some looked back in time and recalled the old, colorful, vibrant society that had existed in the not-too-dim past. They remembered their history before the coming of the tall ships with their strangers from strange lands. They felt that in a sense the advent of statehood bound them closer to a brash young nation that carried them farther from their beginnings. These few looked out and wept.

The statehood boom changed the face of Hawai'i in dramatic ways. Now the Islands were split into four counties. The city limits of Honolulu stretched to encompass the Islands at the northwest end of the chain – sixteen hundred miles of islands, shoals, rocks, and sandbars. Honolulu gave birth to numerous American-style high-rises, right down to the air-conditioning and closed windows that shut out the trade winds. Freeways began their sinuous course across O'ahu.

More green space was covered by concrete, and the population rocketed skyward, from around two hundred fifty thousand in the mid-1950s to more than

Democrat parade profile, June 1963 – President John F. Kennedy; Hawai'i Governor (and statehood architect) John A. Burns; highly decorated 442nd Regimental Combat Team veteran and U.S. Senator Daniel K. Inouye.

John W. A. "Doc" Buyers took the helm of C. Brewer and Company – Hawai'i's oldest company – 1975.

Side by side – at the 1978 rededication ceremonies, 'Iolani Palace – family members of Hawai'i's last reigning monarch, maka'āinana (commoners), Asian Americans, and others (left to right): Edward Kawānanakoa; the Reverend Abraham K. Akaka; kumu hula 'Iolani Luahine; Abigail Kekaulike Kawānanakoa; Governor George R. Ariyoshi; two unidentified women; Regina Kawānanakoa; unidentified man.

Lt. Governor John D. Waihe'e, 1982, became Hawai'i's first elected governor of Hawaiian descent in 1986.

Myron B. "Pinky" Thompson, 1924-2001. Called "a lion in service to his fellow Hawaiians and an icon in the renaissance of that native culture," his areas of leadership centered around education, health, social services, and land use.

a million by 1990. There were positive developments amid the building boom. The East-West Center for Technical and Cultural Interchange became a reality instead of a dream, and attracted scholars from all over the world. The University of Hawai'i took on more autonomy even as it grew in stature and numbers. Heightened competition meant that local business began to diversify. Tourism continued to grow and to be the engine that drove the local economy. Honolulu boasted a zoo, a symphony, an opera season, a famous museum, and an art academy. The neighbor Islands began to blossom as tourism increased in places that had been somnolent—some say underdeveloped—and opulent resorts sprang up on the dark lava coastlines.

Slowly, but with a kind of gentle certainty, high-tech industries began to find their way to the Islands. Maui developed an extensive high-tech park. Industries that could segue into high-tech operations began to do so, receiving grants along the way and proving that such technology could work well in the Islands. Satellites linked Hawai'i with major cities around the world, and if some of the romance of Hawai'i was gone, some modern advantages had arrived.

In downtown Honolulu, *kama'āina* businessmen who had at first reacted badly to the infusion of Mainland ideas and Mainland capital now began to take advantage of the technology and the rush of new prospects. Many of the old guard retired or were replaced, and a new and adventurous spirit seized the business community so that Honolulu firms could begin to export ideas and services. Honolulu-trained technicians turned up in many exotic parts of the world, particularly in places where sugar and pineapple were grown. Some business leaders found that Hawai'i's mid-Pacific location, with its favorable time zone, could be an asset in dealing with the economies of Asia as well as the Mainland. The Islands became a linkage point and all at once began to live up to their nickname as the Crossroads of the Pacific.

In the midst of all this the ordinary people of Hawai'i—the farmers and fishermen, the housewives and shopkeepers, the construction workers and flower growers—all came to grips with the new ways and the new economy. They went about their business with aplomb, enjoying the world's greatest climate even as they had to work hard to maintain a decent standard of living in one of the world's most expensive places. The Islands grew to have the highest percentage of working wives in the nation. Taxes were among the highest, and it was a fortunate couple who could afford to buy a home. The land knew droughts and the economy knew recessions, sugar and pineapple industries declined, but it would have been difficult to find Hawai'i citizens who would willingly live elsewhere. Partly it was the climate that held them, partly the strong sense of family, and partly the beauty of sun-washed lands in a cerulean sea under a vaulting sky.

Mostly what has kept Hawaiian citizens in the Islands is the miracle of mixing, the wonderful melding of races that in turn generates the great tolerance for one another and the appreciation of other cultures and customs. It is true that there are occasional racial incidents with a population of more than a million. But in a real sense the intermarriages and the mixing of diverse races have made for a populace that enjoys the differences among its neighbors.

This is the second of the great epics of Hawai'i, following in the wake of the first great epic of the Polynesian voyages of discovery and colonization. When they stood in the graceful double-hulled canoes and looked on the new land at the apex of the Polynesian Triangle, those old voyagers had no inkling of the civilization that would spring from their discovery. They knew they had found a strange new land replete with phenomena unknown to them—snow and erupting volcanoes—but it was beyond their knowledge and abilities to foresee what the land would generate. They might have been gratified to sense that the Islands one day would be more than a beauteous and busy mid-ocean crossroads; they would be a model for a world in which racial equality and racial acceptance is a prerequisite for world peace.

Governor George R. Ariyoshi, Hawai'i's first governor of Japanese ancestry, signs Festival of Trees Day proclamation, November 30, 1979, with members of The Queen's Medical Center Auxiliary and Queen's President Will J. Henderson.

John D. Bellinger, 1986, leader in community affairs and banking sector – he was with First Hawaiian Bank for 47 years.

Governor Benjamin J. Cayetano – Hawai'i's first governor of Filipino ancestry, 1994-2002.

Kaua'i-born U.S. Senator Spark M. Matsunaga was a Harvard graduate and another highly decorated 442nd Regiment veteran; he also worked tirelessly in community affairs. His special mission – peace.

Gladys Ainoa Brandt – education and community affairs leader; chairwoman emeritus, Board of Regents, University of Hawai'i, 2002.

CHAPTER 14

HULA AND LEI: TRADITIONS CONTINUE

From its original sacred and celebratory use in ancient Hawai'i, *hula* went through many changes. In the 1820s dancing was suppressed and then forbidden under the missionaries. What most people did not realize is that *hula* continued with instruction carried out in secret. While much knowledge was lost forever, remnants of tradition survived. By the 1890s, despite King Kalākaua's earlier encouragement, public *hula* had become disreputable in the eyes of the powerful white government leaders. After the overthrow of the monarchy, *hula* entered a sad period where it was confined to side shows and vaudeville theaters on the continental United States. Non-Hawaiian performers did inauthentic dances considered shocking. Gradually this evolved into less tawdry entertainment that appeared in early films. Also danced by white performers with no *hula* training, it was considered a spicy addition to stories set in the fabled South Pacific.

In time *hula* and Hawaiian-style music became a craze throughout America, with hundreds of songs composed in English for thousands of *'ukulele* players all across the country. The idea of Hawai'i, linked to fantasies of *hula* girls welcoming all visitors, was fixed in the minds of people far and wide. Few could afford a trip to the islands, until World War II brought an enormous influx of soldiers bound for military action in the South Pacific. Into the late 1950s, *hula* was fun, light entertainment seen in hugely popular Waikīkī hotel floor shows. Hawaiians embraced this form of dance, called *hapa-haole* (half foreign), and many became famous performers and recording artists. However, interest in older, authentic styles of *hula* emerged. As if out of hiding, Hawaiians who had guarded ancient traditions, began to appear.

In 1962, the Merrie Monarch Festival was founded, a small start to what developed into a revolution of dance in Hawai'i. Named for the beloved monarch Kalākaua, the Festival celebrated modern *hula* but importantly, brought back *kahiko*, ancient styles of dance not seen in public for over a hundred years. During the 1970s, the Hawaiian Renaissance saw an explosion of scholarship and choreography true to the origins of *hula* in the Islands. *Hula* schools, *hālau*, increased year by year, devoted to bringing authenticity to costumes, chanting and dance implements. Other major annual *hula* events include the Kamehameha Hula Competition and the noncompetitive Prince Lot Hula Festival

LEFT: Through the Merrie Monarch Festival, *hula kahiko* (ancient-style dance) has undergone a powerful revival. This costume replicates *kapa* (bark cloth) and the dancer's adornments are authentic.

held each summer at Moanalua, O'ahu, on a site where *hula* was performed in ancient times.

Today this proud tradition continues to inspire residents and visitors who flock to Hawai'i from all over the world. Thousands of *hālau* now exist in Japan, Mexico, the continental U.S., and as far away as Europe.

The revival of male *hula*, particularly associated with warriors, is an exciting addition to any performance of ancient-style dance.

This focused young dancer represents the concentration and discipline required for many varieties of *hula* – along with the fun of dancing.

By the 1920s and 1930s the idea of *hula* was so seductive that young women with no connection to *hula* liked to dress up in *hula* costume. By then skirts were usually "grass" or cellophane.

During World War II *hula* was a huge hit with servicemen. *Ti*-leaf skirts gained popularity in the 1940s and remain so in the 21st century.

Along with *hula*, in the eyes of the world the *lei* has come to symbolize Hawai'i. This beautiful ancient tradition goes back to pre-Contact times. Flowers were celebrated in chants and had mythic qualities associated with love, respect, and honoring high chiefs. A *lei* could also be made of fragrant vines, leaves, and was worn as headbands, wristlets and anklets. Missionaries saw this as frivolous decoration, particularly for the association with love-making. Yet flowers were always abundant and both men and women often went out daily with at least a blossom, or several, in their hair.

By the time visitors to Hawai'i began arriving regularly, they were delighted to receive welcoming "necklaces" of fresh, fragrant flowers. Soon this developed into a job for hard-pressed Hawaiians, who set up *lei* stands at the harbor and in downtown Honolulu. Flowers from elsewhere had taken root in the islands and anything bright and sweet-smelling was used. A typical price for a *lei* of the soft, yellow *puakenikeni* was a dime.

The Aloha Day parade was established in 1927 and grew into a lavish annual event. Floats, headdresses and people were decorated in celebration of Hawai'i's many kinds of flowers. This evolved into a continuing tradition of May Day pageants held at schools where everyone wore a *lei*, and honored the past with costumed chiefs and royalty. Today the City and County of Honolulu sponsors a contest, which inspires newly created *lei* designs each year. In Kapi'olani Park the best traditional and new styles are honored. A *lei*, or several, is a necessity for school graduations, political events, birthday celebrations, hospital visits, and arriving and leaving the islands.

Lei sellers, c. 1901. As late as the 1950s *lei* sellers in the Mō'ili'ili area of Honolulu habitually added a few extra – and free – flowers to any purchase.

Political campaigns always had plenty of *lei*. This 1915 campaign junket included (left to right): Representative Carter Glass; Speaker Holstein, House of Representatives (Hawai'i); and Hawai'i Delegate to Congress Prince Jonah Kūhiō Kalaniana'ole.

A Christmas *lei*, 1916 – The Queen's Hospital nurses photographed after a carol serenade for patients.

In Hawai'i, May Day is indeed Lei Day. Of course, no one is too young to celebrate.

The heroic bronze-gilded statue of Kamehameha the Great, in front of Ali'iōlani Hale on King Street in Honolulu, becomes spectacular when draped with dozens of 20-foot *lei* for each Kamehameha Day, 1980.

A great variety of flowers are used for *lei*, some native, others originated in Southeast Asia or elsewhere, and became local favorites.

VOLCANO ERUPTIONS AND TSUNAMI

The give and take of nature is nowhere more impressively illustrated than in Hawai'i. The dynamic action of volcano eruptions shows almost simultaneous destruction and creation of new land. Hawaiians of old developed wonderfully creative legends and *mele* about the phenomenon, evidence of their knowledge that the Hawai'i archipelago was formed by volcanic action in a specific sequence. The famous volcano goddess was known as *Pele-honua-mea* (Pele-the-sacred-earth-person). She was "greatly loved in spite of her bad temper."

While all of Hawai'i's islands are of volcanic origin, the volcanoes on the Island of Hawai'i (the youngest island) include two of the world's most active – Mauna Loa and Kīlauea. There are five; Kohala, the oldest, reveals the greatest erosion. The dormant Mauna Kea erupted last about 4,500 years ago. Still considered active, Hualālai erupts at about 250-year intervals, the most recent being 1801. Mauna Loa is expected to erupt frequently throughout the foreseeable future. Kīlauea, Hawai'i Island's youngest emerged volcano, continues in an eruption that began January 3, 1983 – and the ongoing eruption attracts thousands of onlookers every year. As recently as May 2013, new warnings were issued to kayakers getting too close to the roaring, steaming coastline where lava enters the sea. Deep under the ocean off the southern coast of Hawai'i, Lō'ihi Volcano slowly builds a mass above the floor of the sea, preparing to emerge as Hawai'i's newest island in about 60,000 years.

Eruption of Mauna Loa advancing on Ho'ōpūloa Landing; height of flow – 50 feet; width – 1,500 feet. April 19, 1926.

Alexander Lancaster, African-American and Cherokee, the "first guide to the volcano," takes a break at Kilauea Crater.

A slow-moving avalanche of lava in 1926, with a man on the right between the car and the fiery flow.

Spectacular lava fountains can be seen for at least a mile, and provide a far-reaching glow at night. This sight is a Big Island specialty, but constantly changing, and can cause dramatic destruction.

Hawaiians call devastation from the sea *kai 'e'e or hō'e'e*. The long-standing, inaccurate English version is "tidal wave." The internationally accepted designation is the Japanese word tsunami (harbor wave) to label a series of rapidly moving ocean water generated by:

1. the sudden rise or fall of a section of Earth's crust below or near the ocean (earthquake);
2. volcanic activity; or
3. a landslide occurring below or above the ocean surface.

These seismic events produce extremely long wavelengths and may travel thousands of miles at the speed of a jet plane. As they approach shallower waters near shorelines, they slow down, resulting in an increase in wave height and destructive power. Though a tsunami is imperceptible in the open ocean, the shore onslaught is sudden and without warning, save for receding waters immediately preceding the first wave. On shore, the deluge – which may strike at 30 miles per hour – is perceived not as a breaking wave but as a series of surges, typically arriving 5 to 15 minutes apart. Usually "the third or fourth wave is the highest, with ten or more significant waves arriving over a period of several hours." This out-of-bounds sea may strike at heights exceeding 30 feet and may travel inland for a mile or more.

Hawai'i is exposed to tsunamis generated around the Pacific Ocean's fault zones known as the "Rim of Fire." On record since the first recorded tsunami to strike Hawai'i (1819, leading to 46 fatalities) is a total of 86 events, 15 causing moderate or greater damage. In addition to locally generated disturbances, waves reaching Hawai'i have originated in South America, Kamchatka, and the Aleutian Islands.

Historically, Hilo – on the Big Island of Hawai'i – has been distressingly vulnerable. On April 1, 1946, a tsunami generated in the Aleutian Islands arrived without warning as a series of three waves, reportedly of heights up to 35 feet above sea level, causing 83 deaths.

From Chile, in 1960, Hilo received a second massively destructive hit. The surge made contact at speeds reported at 40 miles per hour in heights up to 35 feet. Lives lost – 61. The last major tsunami to reach Hawai'i was in 1964, generated by a massive earthquake in Alaska. The death toll reached from Alaska to California and Chile, but this time when the tsunami came ashore in the Hawaiian Islands, no lives were lost.

Coming ashore like a massive high-speed rising tide, the wave engulfs Pu'umaile Hospital grounds, Hilo, April 1, 1946.

Using technology brought to the fore during World War II, a warning system was developed. The newest version is in place under the direction of the Pacific Tsunami Warning Center of the National Oceanic and Atmospheric Administration at 'Ewa Beach on O'ahu, serving Hawai'i and 25 countries of the Pacific Rim. Hawai'i Civil Defense conducts regular tests of early warning sirens, and news of earthquakes throughout the Pacific is broadcast by radio and spread over the internet.

The waterfront at Hilo, on Hawai'i Island, sustained the heaviest damage of the April 1, 1946, tsunami. Hilo lost 83 lives.

On Kaua'i, April 1, 1946, property damage included the taro farm of this couple.

CHAPTER 15

BUILDING FOR THE FUTURE

In the second half of the 20th century, several factors converged to result in a spectacular building boom and the transformation of Honolulu from a laid-back agrarian territorial outpost (with sugar, pineapple, and the federal government sustaining the Islands' economy) to the metropolitan center of a world-renowned visitor destination area. Pent-up demand for construction, following four years of no construction during World War II, increased awareness of the Islands. On the continental U.S. a burgeoning middle class ripe for travel also contributed to this phenomenon. In 1959 when Hawai'i was granted statehood, the first jet flights to the Islands were inaugurated, bringing more visitors than there were hotel rooms. Five airlines complained of turning away bookings for lack of rooms. When Pan Am's Willis G. Lipscomb predicted, "You have a tourist industry that could come from obscurity to eclipse all other industries in Hawai'i," it sounded less than realistic. Yet, it was the future.

In the spirit of the times – Windward City Shopping Center, an exuberant celebration of Hawaiian motifs, 1959.

LEFT: Gateway to Waikīkī – the award-winning Hawai'i Convention Center; its fabric sails a metaphor for the sails of ancient voyaging canoes, establishing the Islands as the place of the "people of the canoe."

Ala Moana Shopping Center began construction in 1966, then the "world's largest modern shopping center," and has expanded ever since.

Waikīkī – the one and a half mile crescent of hotels that keeps Hawai'i's visitor industry vibrant; the state's leading attraction.

By the year 2000, and continuing to the present, buildings of all kinds kept on transforming Honolulu as well as towns on the outer islands. Grand hotels now line the south coast of Maui. Time-share condominiums have sprung up from Hawai'i Island to the shores of Kaua'i on the northern end of the chain. The expansion of Ala Moana Shopping Center includes international luxury stores. Restaurants feature world-famous chefs. Film crews for national television shows come regularly to film the latest hit series. New churches and even Hindu temples are constructed for an influx of residents from abroad. Interisland travel is at an all-time high. As the global economy rises and falls, and rises again, Hawai'i remains a beloved destination.

VOYAGING: THE PAST BECOMES THE FUTURE

In 1976, Hawai'i astonished the world with a voyage that rewrote history. The echoes of this are heard in the present, and the changes it brought continue to move forward in the 21st century. During the Hawaiian Renaissance of the 1960s and 70s, Native Hawaiian scholars and activists were inspired to recreate the feats of their ancestors. This involved the settlement voyages of more than a thousand years before, from a distance of over two thousand miles away in the South Pacific. That meant constructing a large ocean-voyaging double canoe to sail through storms without a compass, radio, or modern communication of any kind. However, all knowledge of Polynesian star navigation had disappeared centuries ago. No museum had an ocean-voyaging canoe. Early building efforts were a struggle as a few traditional canoe builders worked from historical blueprints made by officers on the ships of Captain Cook. The project lacked funding and was derided as a hopeless dream. Prototypes were still made, tested, and the Polynesian Voyaging Society was founded on a lean budget. Those at its center were driven by the myths, legends and ancient chants that documented a rich legacy of heroic travel.

When a traditional Polynesian star navigator was discovered on a remote island far to the West, canoe builders in Hawai'i felt renewed hope. After long training and creating navigation techniques for the unfamiliar ocean of the South Pacific, the voyaging canoe *Hōkūle'a* was launched. Its name, meaning Star of Gladness, would prove to the world that Polynesians were the greatest long-distance travelers of all time. *Hōkūle'a's* safe arrival in Tahiti was reported in the international press. Readers from America to Europe to Asia and beyond were filled with admiration at the feat: powered only by wind and guided by the stars, clouds, and observing wave swells and currents, *Hōkūle'a* and its crew demonstrated that history textbooks were wrong about migration patterns. Hawai'i's myths, legends and ancient chants were vindicated.

Hōkūle'a went on to become a key role in education throughout Polynesia. More long voyages to Pacific Island nations sparked a revival of traditional canoe building and sailing. In 1973 there were no Polynesian voyaging canoes; by 2000, there were six, with more under construction in Hawai'i and elsewhere. What began as a scientific experiment to build a replica of a traditional voyaging canoe, for a one-time sail to Tahiti, became a catalyst for a generation of cultural renewal. It is also an enduring symbol of the richness of Hawaiian culture and seafaring heritage that links all of the peoples of Polynesia. Festivals for traditional sailing now attract a variety of ocean-going canoes that travel thousands of miles to Tahiti, Micronesia, New Zealand, Easter Island. Other far-flung locations are planned for joyful reunions of men and women who have rediscovered their heroic past.

In April of 2000, at the 25th anniversary of the launching of *Hōkūle'a*, the late Myron Thompson, president of the Polynesian Voyaging Society emphasized its value to the present and the years to come. He set the navigational direction for the 21st century as "Mālama Hawai'i: Navigating the Future" – take care of Hawai'i and her people, that they may thrive always. Following are excerpts from his message:

> *Hōkūle'a has now sailed more than 100,000 miles. We have traveled to every point in the vast Polynesian Triangle, reunifying kin and celebrating our shared voyaging heritage. Our canoe family has even grown to include the native people of Alaska. Our educational programs have reached more than half a million students across the state.*
>
> *Our canoe family is large and knows no ethnic or economic boundaries – we are bound together by our deep love of Hawai'i and our commitment of ensuring that the Hawai'i we know and love today is a place worthy of leaving to our children and those that will follow them. Our Mālama Hawai'i vision is that Hawai'i, our island home, be a place where the land and sea are cared for and communities are healthy and safe for all people.*

"With the backlight of the rising sun, you read the face of the sea ... Without the moon, the only way you can navigate in the middle of the day is by the direction of the waves."
– Nainoa Thompson, Master Navigator.

RIGHT: The voyaging canoe *Hawai'i Loa* off the island of Moloka'i, 1995. The double canoe was made from two Sitka spruce logs from Alaska.

The history-making voyaging canoe *Hōkūle'a* in the Kaiwi Channel between O'ahu and Moloka'i.

Strong hands lashing *'iako* (cross beams) of the *Hawai'i Loa* with sennit, which provides strength and flexibility to a canoe's critical stress points.

Hōkūle'a welcomed on her return from the historic voyage to Tahiti, 1976, off Waikīkī.

Restoration of the revered *Hōkūle'a* recalls the visionaries who gave her life, Polynesian Voyaging Society cofounders scholar Ben Finney; waterman Tommy Holmes; artist Herb Kane; Caroline Islander navigator Mau Piailug; scientist Will Kyselka; and community leader Myron Thompson, who provided the information, support, and the inspiration his son Nainoa needed to become Hawai'i's first modern Master Navigator.

Ceremonies, 1995, welcoming the *wa'a* (canoes) from Taiohae, Nuku Hiva, the Marquesas Islands, quite probably the homeland of Hawai'i's original settlers.

'Awa ceremony for the arrival of *Hōkūle'a* on Maui, during her statewide sail, 1997. Hawaiian communities experienced cultural renewal and continue to celebrate the strengths of a racially diverse people.

The vision for the voyage ahead had begun. In one example, PVS collaborated in a two-year program at Wai'anae High School Marine Science Learning Center, "*Ho'olōkahi*: Charting a Course for Life." Students worked together to solve problems on their own aquaculture farm and aboard a voyaging canoe. This integrated "lessons in oceanography, meteorology, astronomy, geography and the cultural heritage of various regions of the island, and (taught) students self-reliance."

In 2002, PVS, with the Department of Education, the University of Hawai'i, and other educational and community partnerships, presented an Ocean Learning Program for high school students. Curriculum merged academic requirements with activities that included traditional navigational skills. Master Navigator and program director Nainoa Thompson defines the methods – learning to read the stars and the waves and developing the senses – as "inner technology." The navigator trained in traditional skills relies on those rather than the "outer technology" of high-tech development, and Thompson believes this has application to living in the contemporary world. His mission in passing on the ancient art is more than sentiment about recalling the past. It arises from his conviction that those youngsters who master "inner technology" will lead our technological progress in the right direction.

For over 30 years knowledge of ancient voyaging techniques has merged with modern technology. Here an early class gets hands-on experience: the Youth of Hawai'i learning the ropes for their voyage through life – together. *E Ola Mau ...* To Thrive Always.

CHAPTER 16

HAWAI'I IN THE 21st CENTURY

The two centuries since Kamehameha unified the Islands have seen great change. Hawai'i today is the result of wars, politics, technology, economic conditions, and marketing techniques. The population now stands at 1.3 million, roughly 40% Asian, 25% Caucasian, 25% two or more races, and 10% Native Hawaiian and other Pacific Islanders. About a quarter of the total is comprised of residents on the many military bases. Due to years of seeking jobs on the continental U.S., more people who identify as Native Hawaiian, about 450,000, now live outside the islands than in Hawai'i. The home population has shifted with an influx of residents from North America and abroad who favor the numerous fine golf courses.

The beautiful sands of Waikīkī and calm, lovely ocean get a special visit from the voyaging canoe *Hōkūlea.*

LEFT: The landmark Royal Hawaiian Hotel, Hawai'i's world-famous "Pink Palace," continues to welcome visitors from around the globe.

141

The visitor industry is the state's largest, a vast network of airlines, hotels, restaurants, stores, car rental companies, shuttle buses, and entertainment ranging from water sports to helicopter tours to zipline rides. Room occupancy rates are front page news. So is weather, although it's predictably excellent and attracts tourists from around the world. Waikīkī, an unsurpassed playground, continues to attract millions of visitors every year. The grand Royal Hawaiian and Moana hotels have undergone extensive renovation. The Hawai'i Convention Center at the other end of Kalākaua Avenue hosts national and international meetings of groups ranging from teachers to scientists to inventors of the newest toys.

In the digital age, Hawai'i is no longer remote and has become home to internet entrepreneurs. Against all odds, its ancient language has returned as charter schools annually increase the number of Hawaiian speakers. Agriculture has again diversified, with boutique farms now growing lavender and vanilla, and making specialties like goat cheese. Taro production is up, but sugar has declined to a remnant plantation on Maui. Pineapple is no longer raised and exported. The Parker Ranch still supports a half dozen *paniolo* who care for herds of prime cattle.

Almost two centuries of intermarriage have given Hawai'i a unique and much-admired population. In *He Mele O Hawai'i*, The Song of Hawai'i, the author put it this way:

Hula traditions are carefully passed on to the younger generation.

The people came together in a way that was miraculous, and not a collective miracle but one that took place individually, in each untrammeled heart. They reached across barriers of color and custom, leaped across the barricades of intolerance to embrace each other in a kind of acceptance that did not seem to be occurring anywhere else. No attempt was made to disguise their differences; rather each of them found something in those dissimilarities to admire and enjoy. It was as if each decided that the other was exotic rather than eccentric, and in surrendering their xenophobia, each found a freedom to associate, to encompass, to love.

Nā Hōkū music awards, Hawai'i Opera Theater, a beloved local event for the world-wide music industry that embraces Hawaiian music.

Both *hula* and the famous music of the Islands have now gone international. The home-grown songs of The Brothers Cazimero and Israel Kamakawiwo'ole (Brudda Iz) are known all over the world. The most recent local star began his rise to fame via YouTube; the *'ukulele* virtuoso Jake Shimabukuro has appeared at Carnegie Hall and sparked a new generation of listeners. Stage performances in Honolulu are enriched by Hawai'i Opera Theater, backed by the Honolulu Symphony, founded in 1900. Community-based Diamond Head Theater, active since 1915 and one of the oldest in the United States, is a beloved local institution.

Commitment to the fine arts is as strong as ever. The expanded and renovated Bishop Museum remains the repository for exhibits of Hawai'i's ancient treasures, including the fabulous feather cloaks and helmets of the ruling chiefs. The mission of other organizations forms a strong community-wide support base. The Honolulu Academy of Arts, founded in 1927 by Anna Rice Cooke, daughter of New England missionaries, stated her legacy was:

> … *That our children of many nationalities and races, born far from the centers of art, may receive an intimation of their own cultural legacy and wake to the ideals embodied in the arts of their neighbors … may perceive a foundation on which a new culture, enriched by the old strains, may be built in these islands.*

In the arena of 21st century sports, and as the birthplace of surfing, Hawai'i hosts the annual Vans Triple Crown of Surfing. This month-long professional competition takes place on O'ahu's famed North Shore, with one women's event

Honolulu Theater for Youth, founded half a century ago, features the best of contemporary children's theater.

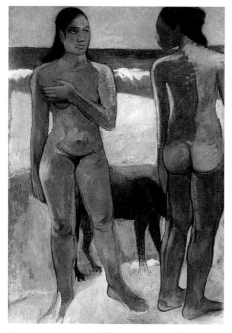

"Two Nudes on a Tahitian Beach," by Paul Gauguin, 1894, selected in 1931 for the Honolulu Academy of Arts by its founder before Gauguin was well known.

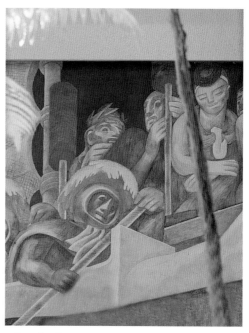

"The Chief's Canoe," fresco by Jean Charlot, Paris-born artist who arrived in 1949 to teach at the University of Hawai'i, his home base the rest of his life. He earned international acclaim for a bold, sculptural style.

on Maui. Its enormous popularity has created spin-off industries not only in surfboards and equipment, but the clothing and accessories that make fans feel part of the action. Surfing and water sports are often at the center of the newest hit series seen on the home screen. Major movie companies also work in the islands throughout the year.

Finally, what of the Hawaiians, the sons and daughters of the first inhabitants? Notwithstanding King Kalākaua's fears, their voices did not fall silent, nor have they disappeared. All the immigrant groups that came after the Polynesians have played out their lives against the backdrop of Hawaiian culture and customs. The considerable intermarriages disseminated many attitudes, practices, and ideals that might otherwise have been lost. The very rocks, hills, and streams of the Islands seem to speak with the voices of the first people. The call for a form of sovereignty is an outgrowth of a newfound pride of being Hawaiian, and heralds a strong voice as the community moves into the future. The ongoing cultural renaissance cuts across ethnic and age groups to include all in the spirit of *aloha*.

Triple Crown of Surfing contest, a stunning display of skills.

The annual North Shore competition attracts crowds and competitors from South Africa to Brazil to Japan and beyond.

APPENDIX

Image Editor's Acknowledgments

The joy of working on this project was about "the hunt" – for images and information – and "discovery." Even familiar images harbor unfamiliar facts. The finding is the fun. The fun is made possible and greatly enhanced by the people one works with and relies upon – from the project team to the community whose mission it is to preserve and manage Hawai'i's historical resources; from historians, archivists, research specialists, and collectors to Hawaiian language experts, writers and editors, artists, secretaries, lab technicians, graphic designers, and numerous generous people who happen to have a needed photograph or bit of information they are willing to contribute to the work in progress; and the foundation of it all – the photographers.

To the project team – Scott Stone, DeSoto Brown, Rhoda Hackler, and Jan Stenberg – goes a full measure of appreciation.

Luella Kurkiian, branch chief for historical records, Hawai'i State Archives, and every member of her staff – Jason Achiu, Ann Cecil, Marlene Donovan, Sandra Harms, Allen Hoof, Patricia Lai, Deborah Lee, Victoria Nihi, and Gina Vergara-Bautista – deserve thanks for their more than a year of assistance.

Outstanding among scores of other helpful contributors were: Judy Bowman, Monte Costa, Page Costa, Tony Costa, Lorraine Dove, Nancy Hedemann, Stuart Ho, Olivier Koning, Jim Manke, Shirley Maxfield, David Montesino, Pepi Nieva, Jay Otani, John Rampage, Mary Richards, Carol Silva, Howard Wolff, Pamela Ho Wong, and David Yamada.

It is a pleasure to acknowledge these institutions, organizations, and firms that in one way or another played a valuable role in the process leading to the completion of this work: Hawai'i Academy of Recording Arts; Aloha Week Festivals; Bishop Museum; Camera Hawai'i; Diamond Head Theatre; General Growth Properties, Inc.; Hawaiian Historical Society; Honolulu Academy of Arts; *The Honolulu Advertiser*; Honolulu Theatre for Youth; Honolulu Symphony; Kamehameha Schools; La Pietra/Hawai'i School for Girls; Library of Hawai'i; Office of the Governor/State of Hawai'i; Office of the President/University of Hawai'i; Photo Hawai'i; U.S. Army Museum; WATG Architects.

References

Beckwith, Martha Warren. *The Kumulipo: A Hawaiian Creation Chant*. Honolulu: University of Hawai'i Press, 1951.

Bingham, Hiram. *A Residency of Twenty-one Years in the Sandwich Islands*. New York: Praeger, 1969.

Bird, Isabella L. *Six Months in the Sandwich Islands*. Honolulu: University of Hawai'i Press for Friends of the Library of Hawai'i, 1964.

Daggett, the Honorable R. M. Introduction to *King David Kalākaua, Myths and Legends of Hawai'i, by His Hawaiian Majesty King David Kalākaua*. Rutland, V.T., and Tokyo: Charles E. Tuttle Company, 1972.

Ellis, William. *Journal of William Ellis*. Rutland, V.T., and Tokyo: Charles E. Tuttle, 1979.

MacLean, Alistair. *Captain Cook*. Garden City, N.Y.: Doubleday & Company, 1972.

Stone, Scott C. S. *He Mele O Hawai'i*. Los Angeles: Jostens Publishing Group, 1993.

Twain, Mark. *Mark Twain in Hawai'i: Roughing It in the Sandwich Islands*. Foreword by A. Grove Day. Honolulu, Mutual, 1990.

Photo Credits

All photos are from the Hawai'i State
Archives unless otherwise noted
below.

IHP = Island Heritage Publishing
HHS = Hawaiian Historic Society

Pp. 4-5
©Monte Costa

Pp. 6-7
Costa Collection

P. 31
HHS (map)

P. 32
Derby del. C. Taylor, S.C.

Pp. 48-49
Costa Collection

P. 65
Costa Collection

P. 93
Costa Collection (top right)

P. 94
Costa Collection (left, bottom right)

P. 100
Bishop Museum/United Japanese
    Society (top)
Courtesy of Jay Otani (bottom)

P. 101
U.S. Army Museum of Hawai'i

P. 102
Courtesy of Nancy Hedemann, Robert
    Huber Collection (bottom)

P. 103
Costa Collection

P. 111
Costa Collection

P. 112
Costa Collection (bottom left)

P. 116
Costa Collection (bottom left)
Mazeppa Costa (bottom right)

P. 117
The Honolulu Advertiser/Monte Costa
    (left)
©Monte Costa (right)

P. 119
Mazeppa Costa (top and middle right)
Costa Collection (middle left, middle,
    bottom)

Pp. 120, 122
IHP

P. 124
Costa Collection, The Queen's
    Medical Center (bottom)

P. 125
Ann Cecil

P. 130
Ann Cecil

P. 131
WATG Architects/R. Wenkam Photo

P. 132
© General Growth Properties, Inc. (top)
Ann Cecil (bottom)

Pp. 134-139
©Monte Costa

Pp. 140-142
Ann Cecil

P. 143
Hawai'i Academy of Recording Arts

P. 144
Honolulu Theatre for Youth/Nieva
        Photo (top)
Honolulu Academy of Arts
        (bottom left)
Olivier Koning (bottom right)

P. 145
Ann Cecil

Selective Bibliography

Allen Gwenfred, *Hawai'i's War Years 1941-1946* (Honolulu: University of Hawai'i Press, 1950), pp. 363-364.

Allen Helen G., *The Betrayal of Lili'uokalani: Last Queen of Hawai'i 1838-1917* (Honolulu: Mutual Publishing, 1982), p. 36.

Ambrose Greg, "Ho'olōkahi," *Honolulu Star-Bulletin* (April 29, 1996).

Black John M., ed., *Hawai'i: Ka 'oihana hōkele, The History of Hawai'i's Hotel Industry 1840-1990* (Honolulu: Trade Publishing Co., 1990), pp. 50-74, 82-110.

Brower Kenneth, "Pacific Wayfinders," Herter, *Discovery: The Hawaiian Odyssey*, p. 18.

Chenoweth Candace A. and Napier A. Kam, *Shuffleboard Pilots: The History of the Women's Air Raid Defense in Hawai'i, 1941-1945* (Honolulu: Arizona Memorial Museum Association, 1991), pp. 63-64.

Cooke Mary, *To Raise a Nation* (Kingsport, T.N.: Hawaiian Mission Children's Society, 1970), pp. 25-31.

Costa Mazeppa King, "Dance in the Society and Hawaiian Islands, as presented by the Early Writers, 1767-1842," M.A. thesis, University of Hawai'i, 1951, pp. 96-97.

Curtis George, "Tsunamis," *Atlas of Hawai'i, Third Edition*, Soian P. Juvik and James O. Juvik, eds. (Honolulu: University of Hawai'i Press, 1998), pp. 76-78.

Daws Gavan, *Shoal of Time: A History of the Hawaiian Islands* (Honolulu: The University Press of Hawai'i, 1968).

Ellis William, *Journal of William Ellis: A Narrative of a Tour Through Hawai'i in 1823* (Honolulu: Hawaiian Gazette Co., Ltd., 1917).

Feher Joseph, Joesting Edward, and Bushnell O. A., *Hawai'i: A Pictorial History* (Honolulu: Bishop Museum Press, 1969), pp. 376-379.

Finney Ben, *Voyage of Rediscovery* (Berkeley/Los Angeles/London: University of California Press, 1994), p. 226.

Handy E. S. Craighill and Pukui Mary Kawena, *The Polynesian Family System in Ka-u, Hawai'i* (Rutland, V.T., and Tokyo: Charles E. Tuttle Company, 1972), pp. 2-9.

Hartwell Jay, *Nā Mamo: Hawaiian People Today* (Honolulu: 'Ai Pōhaku Press, 1996), pp. 31-33.

Hibbard Don and Franzen David, *The View from Diamond Head: Royal Residence to Urban Resort* (Honolulu: Editions Limited, 1986), pp. 2-17.

Hiroa Te Rangi (Peter H. Buck), *Arts and Crafts of Hawai'i VII, Fishing* (Honolulu: Bishop Museum Press, 1964), p. 286.

Holmes Tommy, *The Hawaiian Canoe* (Honolulu: Editions Limited, 1981).

Hopkins Jerry, *The Hula* (Apa Productions [HK] Ltd.: 1982), p. 17.

Judd II Albert F., "Introduction, From the 1937 Edition," *Missionary Album: Sesquicentennial Edition 1820-1970,* Bernice Judd, advisor, and committee (Honolulu: Hawaiian Mission Children's Society, 1969), p. 3.

Kaeppler Adrienne L., *Polynesian Dance* (Honolulu: Alpha Delta Kappa Hawai'i, 1983).

Kamakau Samuel Manaiakalani, *The Works of the People of Old: No Ahana a ka Po'e Kahiko* (Honolulu: Bishop Museum Press, 1976), p. 59.

Krauss Bob, "Academy benefactor a legend," *Honolulu Advertiser* (January 16, 2002).

Kuykendall Ralph S. and Day A. Grove, *Hawai'i: A History* (Englewood Cliffs, N.J.: Prentice Hall, Inc., 1948).

Lili'uokalani, *Hawai'i's Story By Hawai'i's Queen* (Boston: Lothrop, Lee & Shepard Co., 1898; reprint, Rutland, V.T., and Tokyo: Charles E. Tuttle Company, 1964).

McDonald Marie A., "Looking Good, Part 1," *Na Paniolo o Hawai'i,* Lynn L. Martin, ed. (Honolulu: The State Foundation on Culture and the Arts, The Honolulu Academy of Arts, 1987) p. 45.

Martin Lynn J., *Traditions We Share* (Honolulu: State Foundation on Culture and the Arts, Honolulu Academy of Arts, 1997), p. 37.

Mitchell Donald D. Kilolani, *Resource Units in Hawaiian Culture* (Honolulu: The Kamehameha Schools Press, 1982), p. 152.

Morris Ray, AIA, "The Hawaiian House," *Hawai'i Architect* (December 1979): p. 15.

Rose Roger G., *Hawai'i: The Royal Isles* (Honolulu: Bishop Museum Press, 1980), p. 208.

Scott Edward B., *The Saga of the Sandwich Islands* (Lake Tahoe, N.V.: Sierra-Tahoe Publishing Co., 1968), p. 186.

Silva Carol, "The Secret of Fire," *Spirit of Aloha* [July 1999]. http://www.spiritofaloha.com/place

Silva Noenoe K., "He Kānāwai E Ho'opau I Nā Hula Ku'olo Hawai'i: The Political Economy of Banning the Hula," *Hawaiian Journal of History,* Vol. 34 (2000): p. 33.

Stone Scott C. S., *From a Joyful Heart: The Life and Music of R. Alexander Anderson* (Honolulu: Island Heritage, 2001), pp. 136, 169-172.

Stone Scott C. S., *Honolulu, Heart of Hawai'i* (Tulsa, O.K.: Continental Heritage Press, 1983), p. 109.

The Honolulu Advertiser (December 28, 2001): p. A-18.

Thompson Nainoa, "The Six Senses of the Navigator," in *Discovery: The Hawaiian Odyssey*, Eric Herter, ed. (Honolulu: Bishop Museum Press, 1993), p. 12.

Tregaskis Moana, *Hawai'i*, Fifth Edition (Oakland, C.A.: Compass American Guide, 2001) p. 323.

Tsutsumi Cheryl Chee, "Cherishing a gift across generations," *Honolulu Star-Bulletin* (April 14, 2002).

Yamasaki Edward M., "My 442nd Regimental Combat Team Experience and Thoughts on America Today," *Punahou Bulletin* (Winter 2001): p. 25.